ROLL AND GO

SONGS OF AMERICAN SAILORMEN

COMPILED BY

JOANNA C. COLCORD

WITH INTRODUCTION BY

LINCOLN COLCORD

THE BOBBS-MERRILL COMPANY

PUBLISHERS   INDIANAPOLIS

Printed in the United States of America

PRESS OF
BRAUNWORTH & CO
BOOK MANUFACTURERS
BROOKLYN, N. Y

From a painting by an unknown Chinese artist

BARK HARVARD

on the Edge of a Typhoon in the China Sea

(Part of the compiler's childhood was spent on board this vessel)

To the Memory

of

LINCOLN ALDEN COLCORD

Master Mariner

ACKNOWLEDGMENTS

GRATEFUL acknowledgment is made by the compiler to the many shanty-singers who have helped in the collection of this material, and in particular to Capt. Edward H. Cole, Capt. Frank Seeley, Mr. John Donnelly, U. S. N., and Mr. Harry Perry (better known on all the seven seas as "Jimmy Star").

Also to Mr. J. F. McGinnis for the Lake songs and some others, and to Messrs. George Tripp, Zephaniah Pease, Pemberton Nye, Clifford Ashley, George M. Taber, James K. Waterman and Dr. Robert C. Murphy for help and suggestions on the whaling material.

The courteous permission of authors and publishers is also acknowledged for the inclusion of the following copyrighted material:

The Bellman and Mrs. Emily J. Russell, for "John Cherokee," "Slav Ho," and "Derby Ram," from "Songs of the Chanty-man," by Capt. John Robinson.

Sir Richard Runciman Terry for "Johnny Come Down to Hilo."

James Brown & Sons, Glasgow, for "Boston," from "Ships, Songs and Shanties," by Captain W. B. Whall.

Mr. Cecil Sharp for "Liza Lee" and "Sing Sally O."

Brentano's and Mr. Harry Kemp for the poem "Chanteys."

George H. Doran Co. and Houghton Mifflin Co. for quotations from Miss C. Fox Smith.

Mr. Bill Adams for verses from "Johnny Chantyman."

Governor George E. Beckwith of Sailors' Snug Harbor for permission to reproduce several paintings from the collection of the institution.

INTRODUCTION

DURING the half-century between the War of 1812 and the Civil War, the whole American seaboard was engaged in the most intense and far-reaching maritime activity, and along this narrow strip of the world's foreshore the sailing ship, with dramatic suddenness and inspiration, was brought to the utmost peak of her development. Romance and creative achievement were the daily food of a seafaring race. For a term of years, until other nations had learned to copy our designs, the foreign shipping world stood aghast at what we were doing. The American clipper sailed the seas without a rival, a thing of supreme use and beauty, fulfilling the mind's desire for power and the heart's romantic and passionate aspiration in a degree never before attained by the efforts of man.

Where is the contemporary record of this enterprise? It does not exist, for it was never produced. The men who achieved the marvel, made no literature. They even neglected to save for future generations the complete technical data, the shipyard plans and figures, the lines of measurements of their amazing creations. All that remains of the life-work of Donald McKay and a score of other great ship designers is the little that has been preserved by chance—a few paintings of ships, a few half-models of designs that in their day attested the faith and courage of inventive genius, that revolutionized the art of ship-building and made superlative nautical history. And of the life that went forward with these ships—the work, the ambition, the knowledge, the high incentive, the grave responsibility—all that was striven for and attained, all that romance inspired and fortune vouchsafed, all that it meant to sail and be a seaman— of this there remains scant word.

It is a tragic loss, for now it can never be entirely known. We can only make up in appreciation what we lack of verisimilitude. Yet the ways of human reactions are inscrutable; their benefits, also, run by contradictions. We may not be in the right mood to sustain a merchant marine. But we are historians at last, and have the advantage of a wise perspective. Perhaps out of the ardor of our new-found nautical sentiment may be born that genuine sea literature to which our busy forefathers failed to give their attention—a sea literature commensurate with the ships and men of an epic era, and with America's true history on the sea.

INTRODUCTION

It has been with this thought constantly in mind that I have followed the preparation of the present volume. How significant it is that the first scholarly compilation of shanties and sea songs in America should have waited for a day when hardly a square-rigged vessel flying the American flag remained in the deep water trade! Yet not till now, it would seem, has the reading public shown sufficient interest in nautical affairs to make a collection a publishing possibility.

Whatever may be the book's popular reception, it will fall naturally into place as a link in the development of a genuine American sea literature. Such a work, of an accurate and comprehensive nature, has been needed ever since shantying became a custom on board American ships; why our great shipping era failed to produce it, is more than a mystery and something of a shame. Apparently, no one cared. Such blindness to art and intrinsic merit is inexcusable. For shanties, especially, were the very essence of seafaring life, the rollick and bloom of it, and a practical part, withal, of the work that daily and hourly went forward. They were, at once, a necessary item in the handling of a ship, and a perfect characterization of sailordom. They were a ship's "local color," and as such are utilized in every sea story to-day. One would have expected a collection of shanties to stand beside a treatise on seamanship in every nautical library. Yet so many of our best seamen had no nautical library, and only knew the treatise of experience! At any rate, the collection never was made, and a section of shanty material has been lost beyond recall.

Did a Puritanical convention, I wonder, put its ban on shanties as a low, unliterary form of expression? Were American seamen ashamed of their shanties, or did they merely diregard the importance of the art? It is hard to say. Looking back to the seamen I have known, distinguished ship masters of the last days of square-riggers, I think I can see how it was. All these men had been brought up on shantying, so to speak, knew shanties by heart, heard them used on every hand, and would not have permitted their own ships to be handled without them; yet they would have laughed at the bare idea of putting shanties in a book. The lapse is inexplicable; it touches a rigid twist in the utilitarian mind. It is known only in axiom: "familiarity breeds contempt." What, shanties—a book of those old ribald songs? Why, those are the things we sing at sea! Hoisting topsails, or getting the anchor—just imagine! Who wants to hear such stuff? Some of them aren't even decent; they would give a wrong impression. Better leave them alone; I guess you don't know how bad they are. Thus, with a chuckle, the subject is dismissed, and the opportunity passes.

The opportunity, that is, to collect the whole body of the old shanty and forecastle song material at the time when it was in daily use throughout the American merchant marine. But so swiftly has the sailing ship era passed, that men are yet alive who raised shanties on deep water, or beguiled the hours of the dog watch with native balladry; and sailors retain their seagoing memories until they die. A few years luckily remain to us before the gates of sailing ship tradition permanently close. Thus it is still possible to verify at first hand the bulk of our nautical folk-material; and this main body of it, by virtue of survival among onerous conditions, is probably the best of all that was made and sung.

More than this, it is possible still for a genuine seaman, reared in the sailing ship tradition, to approach the task so long neglected. Such an one is the editor of the present volume. Genuine seamanship is not so much a matter of practice and profession as it is a quality of the heart and mind. It is more a sense and feeling than a conscious design. Many a man who holds his full certificates and commands his own vessel is no genuine seaman; the emergency will test him some day, and find him lacking in the instinctive reactions of judgment and love. On the other hand, many who do not follow the sea as a profession were born genuine seamen, live their lives as genuine seamen, and will remain genuine seamen until they die. The brand is on them, the bent can not be escaped. They see life with a sailor's eyes.

In short, they love the sea, and love gives them an understanding deeper than mere aptitude. I speak of what I know; the editor of this collection is a seaman. To have been born at sea, in the cabin of a sailing ship, among the South Sea Islands, the daughter of a ship master; to be descended from five generations of deep water seamen of the New England coast, masters and builders of square-rigged vessels; to have spent the most of her girlhood at sea, up to the age of eighteen, on board her father's vessel, sailing on China voyages; to have learned from him, in loyalty and devotion, in a setting of ocean days, the subtle and intricate lore of the sea; to have lived constantly during those years in an atmosphere of seafaring, knowing none but seamen, seeing nothing but ships and ports and oceans, concerned only with the fortunes of voyages, hearing no speech but the nautical vernacular; to have felt at home on a ship's deck rather than on dry land; to have gained a working knowledge of the handling of a ship, and acquired an instinctive judgment of her condition; and without thought or affectation, but only in confidence, to have loved storms and dangers for the worth they disclosed in ships and men: to have been the cat's-paw of such a destiny, and that during the closing phase of the sailing ship era, was to become a seaman whether or no. It does not constitute a claim, it states a fact. No human being could pass through such an experience and ever lose the feeling of the sea.

Thus the present volume possesses a unique distinction; a compilation of folk-songs, it is made by one who participated, both by life and inheritance, in the folk movement under discussion. That is to say, the greater number of these shanties and forecastle songs have been verified, especially as to music, from the editor's personal recollection. She remembers the tunes as she used to hear them on shipboard, as they were actually sung by sailors in the American merchant marine of her day. She remembers many points raised by her father, who was a good shantyman himself, a stickler for accuracy, and who had a wonderful memory. In addition, her researches have been made close to the sea, and wide shipping connections have served her in good stead. Where material with which she was not previously familiar has been incorporated in the collection, she has received it largely from the lips of seamen living to-day.

In making the compilation, as will be seen, she has consulted all of the fragmentary American collections of shanties and sea songs heretofore published, and all the available British collections, some of them far from fragmentary. What shanty literature exists, has been overhauled, and all possible value derived from these desk sources. But in its final shape, most of the material in this volume has been put to the test of living memory; and where it differs from forms already recorded, it takes its stand on the ground of actuality. These are the words and tunes as they went on shipboard, in the merchant marine that can legitimately claim shantying for its own. The book is a field-work; in the truest sense of the word, it is an authority. Enough to say that it would have passed muster among shanty-singing seamen.

A solemn thought attaches itself to the memory of an era that has completely passed away. The traffic of deep-water sailing ships is done, and will never return to the seas it crossed and conquered for man. No conceivable circumstance, except the ending of the world, can now bury the knowledge of steam, electric and internal combustion engines, of artificial motive power, which is the foundation of a new industrial age. And with this knowledge, man will never again feel the need of the ancient natural means of water propulsion —the sails which, in a sense, have brought him forward, a long and desperate voyage, out of the dim, remote regions of antiquity. Sails are inefficient now. The world's supplies of coal and oil may in time be exhausted, but as yet the resources of electricity have scarcely been tapped. Even if all the tides and waterfalls were eventually to be harnessed, there would still remain the vast waste energy of the sun, an unknown reservoir of power. The word has been said, and man is wedded for all time to his machinery.

One by one the few remaining deep-water sailing ships are disappearing. They drop away, and are heard of no more. With them goes much that is incalculable. It passes like a high squall sinking beyond the horizon, wind and sea, motion and color, the thunder of a majestic purpose, the lightning of swift ideas—all vanishing to leeward with the tall ship in their midst, done with life and bound for the seas of story. The art of seafaring, the rigorous discipline, the peerless craftsmanship, the full life that was part and parcel of a close tradition, these belonged to the days of sail and to no other. A natural

means of propulsion made natural seamen. But the captain of a steamship **is** only a navigating officer. An amount of mechanical power lies at his command, to be pitted against the elements. If the power is not enough, the elements triumph; the engine, not the man, is master of her fate. Wind and weather make no difference; course are straight lines between port and port. Personal judgment carries little weight. Knowledge and understanding of ships is a waste of time; love of the sea is not worth mentioning. All that made the master of a sailing ship a figure of worth and dignity—the responsibility of a free initiative, the stern necessity for correctness of decision, the realization that the voyage from day to day and from hour to hour, in all its wealth of detail and complexity of form, depended on him alone—this, the aura of ships, their gift of power to the men who sailed them, is incommunicable save where taut canvas spreads and decks run steady in the arms of the wind. It does not come with steam.

The master of a steamship may be all that a sailing ship master was. Many men in steam to-day, in point of fact, were brought up under sail; we are still in the period of transition, when the old training lingers to influence the new enterprise. A man of steam, I repeat, may be all that a sail-man (or sailor), was. But he does not need to be, and in the end, when the last men of sail have died and their influence has departed, he will not be; for men as a class do not rise above the exactions of life. The steamship man is a servant, not a master. He takes orders, not gives them. Authority and responsibility go hand in hand; when one is denied, the other is denied also. Industrial progress has lowered the requirements of seamanship. There is not so much at stake, and there is not so much to be won. The life of steam does not develop men to their full capacity. As for the men who would develop themselves under any circumstances, the men of force and character, the best type of the old-school ship master, they simply are not attracted to the profession. As with the masters, so with the officers and seamen. Seafaring has become a lessened vocation.

Thus we discern at last a great truth—that our secret feeling for sailing ships is based on deeper values than those of sentimental attachment or the perception of beauty. It is based on something very real in life, something so true, of such immense significance, that we hardly dare to face the issue. The sailing ship stood for a sociological achievement of the highest order. She stood for a medium whereby men were brought to their fullest development. She stood for a profession where only merit could endure. She stood for the **real** efficiency of spirit and character. She stood for things that we could not afford to lose. There were days when ships and men advanced together; and the supreme beauty of the craft themselves could only have been a reflection of the life they supported, a life brave and clean and full of satisfaction, a life of labor and love. The men who sailed them seemed prosaic, perhaps; the life to

INTRODUCTION

them seemed rough and ordinary. It was the day's work. Greatness of action never knows itself. But now we see it better. And when we admire the sailing ship in picture or story, feeling a vague regret and uneasiness, it is not altogether the longing for romance and adventure that stirs us, but also the realization, sensed but not wholly understood, that a measure of grace has left us with the ships that have sunk beneath the horizon, that life is not so rich as the servants of our machines, that without knowing it we seem to have let a priceless opportunity fall from our grasp; that ships meant more than materials, and that all is not entirely well with the enterprise that has left them behind.

LINCOLN COLCORD

SEARSPORT, MAINE,
    May, 1924.

THE ILLUSTRATIONS

The illustrations for "Roll and Go" have been chosen to show the development in American wooden-built deep-water ships in the last century. They begin with the *Cambridge,* a bark built before the year 1835, along the lines of the British Indiamen which were then the accepted models of our shipbuilders. Bluff of bow and heavy of stern, they shouldered their way through the water instead of slipping through with a minimum of resistance. Such water-colors as this of the *Cambridge* became very much the fashion in seagoing circles in the early part of the last century, and there were in the Mediterranean ports several well-known families of painters who made a specialty of such ship-portraits, hundreds of which are now gathered in American collections and bring large prices. Unlike most painters of ships in the early days, they always signed their works.

The early packet-ships—the forerunners of our transatlantic liners—were built along much the same lines as the *Cambridge.* But the later ships, like the *Isaac Webb,* which was probably the fastest and best-known of the New York packets, showed the clipper influence, and were built by the same men who invented the clipper ship and first made it famous. The British Admiralty asked permission to "take off the lines" of these new vessels as fast as they came to port; and English shipowners later ordered ships from these same American builders. It is interesting that the picture of the famous Black Ball packet here shown should have been taken from a wood-cut in an old copy of the "London Illustrated News."

The change from cargo-carriers to clippers comes out abruptly in the next pictures of the *Sea Witch,* with her lovely yacht-like lines, and the *Young America* with her three skysail yards aloft and the graceful "sheer" or lift of bow and stern away from the straight horizontal line of the earlier ship-designers. Dismal predictions accompanied the launching of the earlier clippers; they would never stand heavy weather; they would capsize; they would carry so little cargo that their owners would be ruined men. It was a sheer act of faith that sent them down the ways; a faith that was amply justified as speed and not burden-bearing became a profit-making quality. Gradually, however, and by means of repeated experiment, a way was found to combine the two qualities, as in the proud and splendid *Andrew Jackson,* the finest of New York's "medium clippers," shown by her modern painter as she " 'scends" down over the crest of a long deep-sea swell.

After the Civil War, speed was again sacrificed to cargo-carrying, although the sharp, curving "clipper bow" of the American shipbuilder was never abandoned. The picture of the *Mary L. Stone* shows a more full-bodied ship, with a broader and heavier stern than the clippers, and with a return to the straight hull-lines of the earlier builders. But in her spread of canvas and her three skysails she is a clipper still.

With the whalers, speed was never for a moment sought at the expense of cargo-room, and they remained to the last the same squat, full-bodied vessels which the picture shows. In the foreground, a whaleboat is being "laid on" to a harpooned whale, the "harpooneer" with his lance poised ready to administer the *coup de grace,* while the ship waits with main yard aback for the whale to be towed alongside. Other boats in the distance are rowing to attack another of the school; while the distant rolling hills of some island of the South Pacific form the background.

The originals of almost all of these pictures are to be found in the splendid collection at Sailors' Snug Harbor, Staten Island, which seems to be unknown and as yet unvisited by the collectors. None of these pictures has ever been reproduced in the volumes of nautical literature known to the compiler, and there is no history at the Harbor of their having been photographed before. Mainly the gifts of old sea captains and their families, they represent an accretion rather than a deliberate attempt at collecting special sorts of pictures; everything is there together, from an old painting on glass of the packet-ship *New Hampshire,* now flaking away from its background, down to the battleships of the Spanish-American War. And in this mingling of good and bad, of oils, water-colors, old prints and engravings, lies its special charm for the lover of ship pictures.

LIST OF ILLUSTRATIONS

PAGE

BARK HARVARD ....*Frontispiece*

Built by Atkinson & Fillmore in Newburyport, Mass., in 1878. Length 181 feet, breadth 35 feet, depth 21 feet, 1033 tons register. Owned by Foster & Pray of Boston, and commanded by the compiler's father, Captain Lincoln A. Colcord, from 1891 till her loss on Turks Island in 1898.

BARK CAMBRIDGE 2

From an old water-color by Peter Mazzinghi of Leghorn, now in the collection of Sailors' Snug Harbor. An early type of American merchantman, built before 1835. This was probably not the Black Ball packet *Cambridge,* which was ship-rigged, and which in all probability never visited the Mediterranean ports.

PACKET SHIP ISAAC WEBB................................... 10

From a wood-cut in the "London Illustrated News." Built in New York in 1850 by William H. Webb, out of live oak, locust and cedar. Length 188 feet, breadth 40 feet, depth 28 feet, 1300 tons register. She was a fast ship as packets went, and often made the trip to Liverpool in sixteen and seventeen days. She foundered in mid-Atlantic in 1881, with a cargo of iron rails.

"HEAVE A PAWL" 32

From a photograph taken by the compiler, showing the crew of the ship *State of Maine* on the forecastle-head, heaving up anchor in Sunda Straits.

EXTREME CLIPPER SHIP SEA WITCH........................... 40

From a painting in Sailors' Snug Harbor. One of the earliest of the clippers, built by Smith & Dimon, New York, in 1846. Length 170 feet, breadth 33 feet 11 inches, depth 19 feet, 890 tons register. Owned by Howland & Aspinwall, and commanded first by Captain "Bob" Waterman, later by Captain George Frazer. Under the former, she made an unbroken record of seventy-seven days from Canton to New York in 1848; under the latter she beat the clipper fleet from New

York to San Francisco, in 1850, with a record passage of ninety-seven days. This passage was made afterward in shorter time; but in her early days, she was the swiftest and handsomest ship afloat. She was lost on the coast of Cuba in 1856.

CLIPPER SHIP YOUNG AMERICA.................................... 66

From a painting in Sailors' Snug Harbor. Built by William H. Webb, New York, in 1853, for the California trade. Length 236 feet 6 inches, breadth 42 feet, depth 28 feet 6 inches, 1962 tons register. Owned by George Daniels and commanded by Captain David Babcock. She once made the passage from San Francisco to New York in eighty-three days, and on twenty consecutive passages from New York to San Francisco her time averaged one hundred and seventeen days. The painting shows her after she was re-rigged in 1860, with reduced spars and canvas and with double topsails. She long outlived her contemporaries in the California trade, and was sold to the Austrians in 1883. Under her new name, *Miroslav,* she foundered with all hands in 1888.

MEDIUM CLIPPER SHIP ANDREW JACKSON......................... 84

From a painting by J. Stuart Blackton in Sailors' Snug Harbor. Built by Irons & Grinnell, Mystic, Conn., in 1855. Length 222 feet, breadth 40 feet, depth 22 feet, 1679 tons register. Owned by J. H. Brower & Co., and commanded by Captain John E. Williams. Although not of extreme clipper build she rivaled the best in her passages, and once reached San Francisco in eighty-nine days from New York, a record equaled only twice, each time by the famous *Flying Cloud.*

"A DEAD WHALE OR A STOVE BOAT" 102

From a painting in Sailors' Snug Harbor, showing a fleet of sperm whalers after a school of whales.

SHIP MARY L. STONE... 114

From a painting in Sailors' Snug Harbor. Built by Gross & Sawyer in Bath, Maine, in 1874. Length 198 feet, breadth 39 feet, depth 24 feet, 1458 tons register. Owned by De Groot & Peck, New York, and commanded by Captain George Josselyn, later by Captain Andrew Carver. A type of American ship which succeeded the clipper, and which, although lacking the extreme swiftness of the latter, combined grace, speed and seaworthiness with a larger capacity for carrying cargo. She was lost on the island of Formosa, while under the command of Captain William H. Gould, about the year 1895.

"Johnny Parrot, Johnny Parrot! I'll not hear you again,
That old voice of yours a-ringin' down the windy rain,
When the ocean mornin's clearin' an' the gale is past,
An' we're all a-yo-heave-ho-in' by the big main mast.

"Johnny Parrot, Johnny Parrot! I can see 'em now,
Southeast trade-wind seas a-breakin' high above the bow.
I can see the yellow oilskins of a shoutin' crew;
Hear the roarin' of their chanty chorus led by you.

"I can feel the clipper tremble as she lifts her feet,
An' her dainty bows are dancin' down the sea's wide street.
I hear Johnny Parrot singing'——singin' 'Roll an' go,'
An' the sons of forty seaports roarin' 'Yo-heave-ho!' "

BILL ADAMS
(From "Johnny Chantyman")

FOREWORD

IN the old days when American sailing ships still ploughed the seas, it was the custom of their sailors to enliven both their work and their leisure time with song. The songs they used were not, generally speaking, those current and popular ashore at the same period, but were traditional compositions of unknown date and authorship, growing as all folk-song does out of the needs and experience of men. These songs of the sea have in every line of their verses and every bar of their music the distinctive flavor of seafaring. They are of equal interest to students of folk-lore and to those who love the memory of old days spent on blue water; and it is with both in mind that this work has been undertaken.

Shanties were the work-songs of the sea. First, a word about the name itself. Controversy has raged among the small group interested from the student's point of view, as to whether the correct spelling is "shanty" or "chantey"; though it is conceded that only the former spelling represents the proper pronunciation of the word. The upholders of "chantey" claim that the word is a clear derivation from the French word "chanter," to sing. The leader of the opposition is Sir Richard Runciman Terry, who thinks it is derived from the shanties in which the negroes lived who originated so many of these songs, or from the drinking shanties along the Mobile water-front where the sailors picked them up. He says:

"To my mind the strongest argument against the derivation from the French is that the British sailor cultivated the supremest contempt for everything French, and would be the last person to label such a definitely British practice as shanty-singing with a French title. If there had been such a thing in French ships as a labour-song bearing such a far-fetched title as (un) chanté, there might have been a remote possibility of the British sailor adopting the French term in a spirit of sport or derision, but there is no evidence that any such practice, or any such term, achieved any vogue in French ships. As a matter of fact, the Oxford Dictionary (which prints it 'shanty') states that the word never found its way into print until 1869."

Personally, I can not follow this argument. Because the English or American sailor had a low opinion of the French, is no reason that his fancy might not have been captured by the sound of a French word; he was as a matter of fact an inveterate picker-up of foreign phrases. Just as one instance, a common expression of his to describe the extra-competent seaman, the shell-back whose "every hair was a rope-yarn and every drop of his blood Stockholm tar," was "a reg'lar old mattalow." And what is *mattalow* but our old French friend *matelot?* If the sailor would thus borrow from the French tongue this term of high though half-humorous praise, why might he not also borrow the name of his songs? *

But all this is only speculation at best; and the originators of the term have gone, taking with them the clue to its derivation. With them have gone into the shadows many of the finest examples of their songs—as the investigator ruefully learns from scattered allusions in the nautical literature of the early days to shanties that have long vanished from the memory of man. What would lovers of shanties not give to hear "Captain Gone Ashore," "Slapander-gosheka," or "Come Down, You Bunch o' Roses, Come Down"? They were sung once, and their names survive, but there is in all probability no one living to-day who ever heard those tunes lifted to halliards or windless.

But to return to the question of spelling—I am adopting in this book the spelling "shanty" simply because all landsmen who meet the other spelling naturally pronounce it with the "ch" hard as in "church"; a pronunciation which sends a shudder down every seaman's spine. "Chantey" looks better on the page, can not be confused with other meanings of the same word, and in the subtle sense of word-feeling seems to suggest more closely than "shanty" the spirit of a sea-song. Yet all these considerations are far outweighed in a seaman's mind by the horrid possibility of encouraging that hard "ch." In other words, I am deliberately choosing the spelling I least prefer, for purposes of nautical accuracy.

The origin of the practice of shantying has been lost in the unrecorded past. An ancient work, "The Complaynt of Scotland," published in 1549, describes a ship getting under way, and says, "As one cry'd, all the rest cry'd in the same time as it had been an echo." This may have referred not to

---

* Another possible derivation of the word "shanty" comes from the Maine woods. Several songs and ballads of the lumbermen, dating from 1870 or thereabout, have been recently collected and published by Professor Roland P. Gray ("Songs and Ballads of the Maine Lumberjacks": Harvard University Press) and these show that the word "shanty-man" was at that time synonymous with "lumberman."

"Come all you brave shanty boys,"

is a favorite opening line. From other sources, I have learned that the same shanties used at sea were commonly used as work-songs in the lumber-woods up to quite a recent date. This indicates a close connection between the woods and the coast; and without doubt many lumbermen from time to time made sea voyages. The word, as has been noted above, did not come to use at sea till the late '60's or early '70's; and the possibility does not seem remote that, just as the songs were carried from the sea to the woods, so the name may have been brought down from the woods to the sea.

shantying, but to the process of "singing out" or "yo-ho'ing" on a rope, an aid to labor still in use at sea and alongshore.

Patterson says that "Whiskey Johnny," (p. 6) is supposed to have been in use at the time of the Armada, with "malmsey" in the place of whiskey. "A-Roving," (p. 37) appears in Thomas Heywood's "The Rape of Lucrece," which was played in London about 1630. But these may both have been used merely as songs in those early days. There is nothing in their words or in the literature of the times to suggest their use as *shanties*. The best evidence of the antiquity of the practice of shantying is to be found in the short-drag shanty "Haul on the Bowline" (p. 4). This has been a puzzle to some writers on the subject, because on modern square-rigged vessels the bowline is an unimportant rope, used merely to steady the leach of a sail when sailing on the wind. No shanty could ever have been used in handling so light a rope; and as a matter of fact, "Haul on the Bowline" has been used time out of mind for the purpose of sheeting home the fore and main courses. But on the carracks of Elizabethan times, the bowline was the name for what we now call the fore-sheet; and it seems fairly evident from the wording of the modern shanty that it must have been in use for its present purpose, ever since those far-off days.

Dana, in 1834, gives the first description in print of shanty-singing on American ships; and from the high degree of development which he pictures, it is evident that the practice must have been going on for many years. L. G. Carr Laughton, writing in the "Mariner's Mirror," says that shantying on British ships during the eighteenth century suffered greatly from the many wars in which England was engaged during that period. British seamen were impressed into the naval service where no shantying was allowed, their places being taken in the merchant marine by foreign sailors to whom shantying was an unknown and uncongenial practice; and not until the years of peace beginning with 1815 could such a peaceful art as shanty-singing develop in the British merchant marine. By that time, on the evidence of Dana, it must have been well advanced in the young and rapidly growing American merchant marine.

The successive developments of the cotton trade between Liverpool and the Southern States, the growing trade for fur and hides around the Horn into the Pacific, the North American packet trade, bringing its tide of emigration to the United States in the early '40's, the birth of the clipper ship on the western shores of the Atlantic, the gold rush to California in '49, and the tea-clipper trade to the Orient, all meant an enormous increase in ships and men using the sea; and in the heyday of those stirring and prosperous times, the art of shanty-singing was developed to its highest point. From 1850 to the Civil War, steam was just beginning to encroach upon sail, and the eager forthputting of the sailing trades was suffering an unconscious check. Almost imperceptibly, an economic era was changing on the sea. The old shanties were still sung, and even in many instances elaborated upon and improved; but new songs were no longer developed. It is interesting to note that practically all of the shanties to follow in this book (all sung on shipboard as late as the '90's in some form) can be traced in their origins farther back than 1850; and that the latest and in many respects the most romantic development of the American sailing ship era—the trade with the Orient carried on by our splendid medium clippers of the '60's and '70's—is barely mentioned in shanty material and gave rise to no distinctive shanties of its own.

Shanties were practically the exclusive possession of sailors on English or American ships. The fact that most of the published collections have been British, has created with the general shore public the erroneous impression that shantying was a British art, borrowed by the Americans. With the ships of both nations meeting in the ports of all the world, and with sailors mingling freely and shipping indifferently in both English and American bottoms, it would be difficult if not impossible to disentangle the matter of origins; but enough has already been said to show that a well-developed body of shanty material must have existed on American ships at a period when British shantying, in the form in which we know the art, was in its infancy. Undoubtedly the very earliest shanties were of British origin; but equally without doubt the *development* of shanty-singing as such, the art itself as it has resounded up and down the Seven Seas for well-nigh a century, has derived much of its inspiration from the American merchant marine. When we deduct from the whole bulk of shanties which survived the period of the Civil War in both services, all those which clearly had their rise in the cotton trade to the Gulf, in the Western Ocean packet ships, and in the gold rush around the Horn, we have listed the greater number.

It should be pointed out in all fairness, however, (1) that the *forecastle songs,* as I have elected to call those which were sung not as work-songs, but for amusement in the sailor's leisure time, are very largely variants of early English, Irish or Scottish ballads (the common heritage of Britain and America), and (2) that even on American ships, Englishmen or Irishmen, of whom there were always a few in every crew, were admitted to rank ahead of the white Americans as shantymen; though they in turn were far outstripped by the American negroes—the best singers that ever lifted a shanty aboard ship.

It should not be supposed that the musical notation of the airs printed in this collection can any more than feebly portray the effects gained by the real shanty-singers. Not only the music, but the way of singing it was distinctive. A good shantyman embellished the bare bones of the air with grace-notes and flourishes; he flung his voice aloft like a bird to reach a high note, soaring above it, then swooping down upon it with an effortless precision, a careless, jubilant swoop and swing that was irresistible. It was as distinctive a style of singing as that of the Swiss jodler, but it was not jodeling—perish the thought! The good shantyman, untaught and without rules except those of custom, could perform feats of vocalization which were a sheer joy to the listener.

A great deal has been written about the grossness and obscenity of shanties. Gross some of the words undoubtedly were, when the shantyman chose so to improvise them; for the solo part of a shanty was largely "made up" by the shantyman as he went along. But it was a jovial, forthright, almost whole-some obscenity, with no suggestiveness or *double entendre* such as disfigures our music-hall compositions; and it served its turn. The shantyman who could surprise a laugh from the crowd on the rope made the work lighter. And it was never the chorus, roared out in full voice by all hands, which was vulgar, but merely the solo part, audible only to those standing near by.

Every shanty had a "pattern" or central theme, to which the improvised words held pretty closely. Often there might be two or three of these general patterns, or versions, as will be shown later. There was always a set of verses embodying the original idea, which was perfectly fit to print, with perhaps one exception, the notorious "Abel Brown," of which there is no version in any of the published collections I have examined.

In improvising the solo part of a shanty, the leader or shantyman with originality and a reputation to maintain tried not to repeat the same line twice. If his story came to an end before the job was over, he fell back on a series of lines describing the piece of work under way, a common stock of which lines were used for "piecing out" on such occasions. (See "So Handy," p. 28.) In order to start the crowd on the right shanty, he would sometimes sing the chorus through first; and "Lowlands" and some others were always begun in this way. Immediately upon the heels of the last word of the solo—often before the last word was fully enunciated—it was the custom for the crew to swing in loud and strong on the chorus. None of the artfulness of the shanty-man was displayed here; the loudest bellower was the best man on the rope, as long as he kept perfect time.

The following examples of these work-songs of the sea are drawn in part from my own memories of years spent on blue water under sail from 1890 to 1899, mostly on voyages between New York and various ports in the China Sea. In part, they are songs learned from my father, who loved them and sang them well, and whose seagoing began about the year 1874. This makes my versions of the songs later than the "classical" period of shanty-singing, which extended from about 1840 up to the time of the Civil War. I also owe grateful acknowledgment to many shanty-singers still alive, whose names will be found elsewhere, and from whose lips I have taken down many of the songs that follow.

In some few instances, I have printed early versions of the same shanty for purposes of comparison. In a few others, I have quoted outright from other collections shanties which clearly show American influences, but which I have never happened to hear on the sea. In almost no case is the set of words as given in the following pages one that I have heard sung as a complete shanty at any one time. No two shantymen ever sang the same shanty exactly alike, in either the words or the music. As far as the words go, I have borrowed here and there, and fitted together the verses which seemed best to develop the central pattern. As for the music, I can only say that the airs stand here exactly as they were sung on board an American ship in the latter part of the nineteenth century, according to my best recollection.

So far as I have been able to learn, this collection of shanties ánd sea-songs is the first attempt to deal thoroughly with the subject from the American point of view. Admiral Luce, U.S.N., in his volume of "Naval Songs" (Pond, New York), includes a few familiar shanties; but as shanties were never used in the Navy, it is not to be wondered at that his collection of them is far from exhaustive. "The Bellman," a defunct magazine formerly published in Minneapolis, contains in its issues for July and August, 1917, a fine collection of shanties by a British shipmaster, Captain John Robinson. "Sailor Chanties and Cowboy Songs," a small paper-covered volume edited by Charles J. Finger (published by Haldeman-Julius), contains a few shanty-words. During the World War an effort was made to revive shanty-singing in connection with the training schools for merchant seamen, and a collection of some of the old shanties was compiled by Stanton King, U.S.N. Except for a few topical articles that have appeared in the periodical press from time to time during the past thirty or forty years, this practically exhausts the list of sources published in America; and one of these, as has been stated, is of British origin.

Great Britain, on the other hand, has a considerable literature of shanties and sea-songs. In preparing this American anthology, the following English collections have been consulted, and will be referred to as occasion requires:

"Songs of Sea Labour," by F. T. Bullen and W. F. Arnold. *Swan & Co., London.*

"A Sailor's Garland," (words only) by John Masefield. *The Macmillan Co., New York.*

"The Sea's Anthology," (words only) by J. E. Patterson. *George H. Doran, New York.* (Printed in England.)

"Music of the Waters," by Laura A. Smith. *London.*

"English Folk-Chanteys," by Cecil Sharp. *Novello, London.*

"The Shanty Book," by R. R. Terry. *Curwen, London.*

FOREWORD

"Sailor's Songs or Chanties," by Ferris Tozer and F. J. Davis. *Boosey, London.*

"Ships, Sea Songs and Shanties," by W. B. Whall. *Brown, Glasgow.*

Shanties naturally fall into three main divisions on a scale of occupational classification; short-drag shanties, halliard (or halyard) shanties, and windlass or capstan shanties. The form of the shanty for each of these three divisions is quite different, since it is fitted to an altogether different job aboard ship. I have used this natural classification in the following pages as a means of dividing the collection into readable lengths, and also as an aid to the general reader in forming a clear conception of what the shanty stood for and how it was used.

Rather than to disfigure the volume with a mass of foot-notes, I have chosen to arrange my notes on individual shanties in the form of a running text or commentary, the shanties themselves falling into their proper places as the discussion goes forward. This arrangement seems to me by far the most readable method of presenting such an unwieldy body of material; while to print a succession of pages carrying the bare shanties, with scattering foot-notes and a bulky appendix at the end of the volume, would be both an annoyance to the reader and a deliberate sacrifice of one of the main purposes of the work. For it has been as much in the hope of offering a seamanlike collection in every way, a volume of shanties possessing both nautical background and foreground, as to make a technical compilation of American shanty material, that the present work has been undertaken. And a true seaman likes neither foot-notes nor appendices; he wants all of his story as he goes.

J. C. C.

New York,
November, 1923.

ROLL AND GO

I

SHORT-DRAG SHANTIES

IN any study of shanties and shanty-singing, we must inevitably begin with a consideration of the short-drag shanties. These exemplify the simplest and probably the earliest form of the art; they are but a step removed from "Yo-heave-ho'ing." Reference has already been made in the introductory section to the practice of "singing out" as an aid to pulling and hauling at sea. Captain Robert C. Adams, in his fine book "On Board the *Rocket*," now unfortunately out of print, thus describes this forerunner of the shanty:

"In addition to the songs, are the unnamable and unearthly howls and yells that characterize the true sailor, which are only acquired by years of sea service. There is the continuous running solo of 'Way-hey, he, ho, ya,' etc., accompanying the hand-over-hand hoisting of jibs and staysails. Then for short 'swigs' at the halyards, we have such utterances as 'Hey-*lee*, ho-*lip*,' or '*yu*,' the emphasis and pull coming on the italicized syllables, on which the voice is raised a tone. Then comes the more measured 'singing out' for the long and regular pulls at the braces. Each sailor has his own 'howl' peculiar to himself, but, fortunately, only one performs at a time on the same rope. The effect, however, when all hands are on deck at a time, and a dozen ropes are pulled on at once, is most suggestive of Babel."

This is exactly the same thing described by Falconer in the latter part of the eighteenth century, as "a sort of song or howl" by which the sailors of those days aided their work about ship. The first shanties to be developed out of this primitive practice were undoubtedly the so-called "short-drag shanties," a few of which have been preserved and kept in use down to the present day.

These simple forms of the shanty were used where only a few strong pulls were needed, as in boarding tacks and sheets, bunting up a sail in furling, "hauling out" on the weather yardarm in reefing a topsail, or "sweating up" the halliards at the end of a long pull. In the latter process the leading singer, or shantyman, with perhaps the second mate to help him, stood up and pulled on the leading part of the rope, the crew "tallying on" behind the lead-block. A great favorite for "sweating up" was

BONEY

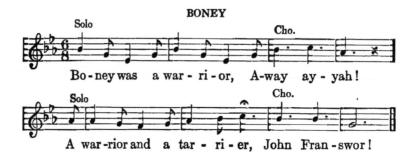

Bo-ney was a war-ri-or, A-way ay-yah!

A war-rior and a tar-ri-er, John Fran-swor!

Boney fought the Roo-shi-ans,
Boney fought the Proo-shi-ans.

Moscow was a-blazing,
And Boney was a-raging.

Boney went to Elbow,
Boney he came back again.

Boney went to Waterloo,
There he got his overthrow.

Boney broke his heart and died
Away in St. Helena.

Drive her, captain, drive her, (twice)

Give her the topgallantsails; *
It's a weary way to Baltimore.

At the last syllable of each chorus, all hands gave a mighty pull, and "brought her home." There were endless verses to this old favorite; and as historical accuracy never troubled the sailor, we have one version in which Boney crosses the Rocky Mountains, and another in which he is sent to St. Helena "all on account of a woman!"

* Pronounced to'gan'l s'ls.

BARQUE CAMBRIDGE. R.R.DOANE MASTER ENTERING THE PORT OF LEGHORN OCTOBER 12 1835.

BARK CAMBRIDGE

A pre-clipper type of American merchantman

Another—consecrated by usage to the sheeting home of the foresail—is

HAUL AWAY, JOE

Oh, once I had an Irish girl, but she was fat and lazy,

And then I had a yeller girl, she nigh druv me crazy,

But now I've got a Yankee girl, and she is just a daisy.

In this shanty, the only pull was on the word "Joe," which was shouted or grunted out rather than sung. In English ships, they sang a longer version:

Once I was in Ireland, digging turf and 'taties
But now I'm on a lime-juice ship, hauling on the braces.

King Louis was the king of France afore the rev-o-lu-shi-on,
But Louis got his head cut off, which spoiled his con-sti-tu-shi-on.

Once I married an Irish girl, and her name was Flannigan,
She stole my money, she stole my clothes, she stole my plate and pannikin.

St. Patrick was a gentleman, he come of dacent people,
He built a church in Dublin town and on it put a steeple.

The oldest of the short-drag shanties is probably "Haul on the Bowline" (pronounced bō-lin). Masefield says of it that it was "certainly in use in the reign of Henry VIII. It is still very popular, though the bowline is no longer the rope it was. It is a slow, stately melody, ending with a jerk as the men fall back on the rope."

HAUL ON THE BOWLINE

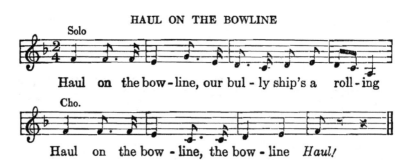

Haul on the bow-line, our bul-ly ship's a roll-ing

Haul on the bow - line, the bow - line *Haul!*

Haul on the bowline, Kitty is my darlin',
Haul on the bowline, Kitty lives at Liverpool,
Haul on the bowline, the old man is a growlin',
Haul on the bowline, it's a far cry to payday,
Haul on the bowline, so early in the morning.

The next shanty was used for only one operation, the "bunting" of a sail in furling; and was sung in chorus throughout, the last syllable, when all hands gave a tremendous lift to the heavy roll of canvas to get it on top of the yard, being simply a yell. Usually only one verse was necessary.

Paddy Doyle was a famous dive-keeper in Liverpool. It is told of him that he kept a cow's horn in the back yard, round which he solemnly marched "green hands," so as to be able to tell a doubting skipper that they had "been three times round the Horn!"

The shanty was doubtless related in the mind of the singers to the sea-superstition that it brings bad luck to leave port with bills unpaid.

PADDY DOYLE

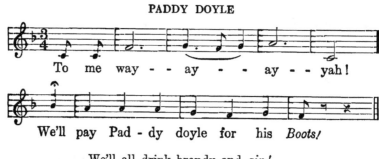

To me way - - ay - - ay - - yah!

We'll pay Pad - dy doyle for his *Boots!*

We'll all drink brandy and *gin!*
We'll all shave under the *chin!*
We'll all throw dirt at the *cook!*

Captain Whall says that the following shanty was also used exclusively in furling sail; but on American ships it was more commonly used for sheets and tacks. "Johnny Boker" is one of the mysterious heroes of shantydom, about whom nothing more is known than his name.

JOHNNY BOKER

Do my John-ny Bo - ker, Come rock and roll me

o - ver; Do my John-ny Bo - ker *do!*

Do, my Johnny Boker, the skipper is a rover,

Do, my Johnny Boker, the mate he's never sober,

Do, my Johnny Boker, the bo'sun is a tailor,

Do, my Johnny Boker, come roll me in the clover.

The words of a popular American shore ballad, "Aunt Jemima's Plaster," were sometimes adapted to this tune:

Last time I met my wife, she wasn't very civil;
So I stuck a plaster on her back and sent her to the devil.

Sheepskin, pitch and beeswax, they make a bully plaster;
The more she tries to get it off, it only sticks the faster.

II

HALLIARD (OR HALYARD) SHANTIES

HALLIARD shanties were used chiefly for the longer and heavier tasks aboard ship, such as hoisting sail, catting the anchor, etc. They are quite regular in form, usually written in common time, with a solo line followed by a chorus of the same length. Two solo lines and two chorus lines make up the stanza. Sometimes the chorus provided for two pulls on the rope; generally, however, for only one. Many of the halliard shanties were used in pumping ship; and sometimes they were used to put life into the crew when tramping round the capstan, though for this use the more elaborate windlass shanties were more common. (See p. 31.)

One of the oldest of the halliard shanties is "Whiskey Johnny." Praise and deprecation of the use of alcohol are about equally mingled in this remarkable human document!

WHISKEY JOHNNY

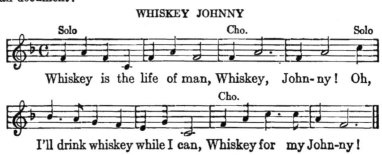

Whiskey is the life of man, Whiskey, John-ny! Oh,
I'll drink whiskey while I can, Whiskey for my John-ny!

O whiskey straight and whiskey strong,
Give me some whiskey and I'll sing you a song.

O whiskey makes me wear old clo'es,
Whiskey gave me a broken nose.

Whiskey killed my poor old dad,
Whiskey druv my mother mad.

If whiskey comes too near my nose,
I tip it up and down she goes.

6

I had a girl, her name was Lize,
She puts whiskey in her pies.

My wife and I can not agree;
She puts whiskey in her tea.

Here comes the cook with the whiskey can,
A glass of grog for every man.

A glass of grog for every man,
And a bottle full for the shantyman.

A group of famous old shanties had their origin in the packet-trade with Liverpool, which developed soon after the close of the War of 1812.

BLOW, BOYS, BLOW

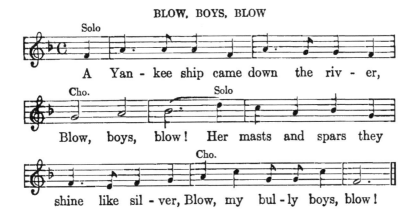

A Yan - kee ship came down the riv - er,
Blow, boys, blow! Her masts and spars they
shine like sil - ver, Blow, my bul - ly boys, blow!

How do you know she's a Yankee liner?
The Stars and Stripes float out behind her.

And who d'you think is the captain of her?
Why, Bully Hayes is the captain of her.

And who d'you think is the mate aboard her?
Santander James is the mate aboard her.

Santander James, he's a rocket from hell, boys,
He'll ride you down as you ride the spanker.

And what d'you think they've got for dinner?
Pickled eels' feet and bullock's liver.

Then blow, my bullies, all together,
Blow, my boys, for better weather.

Blow to-day and blow to-morrow,
And blow for all tars in sorrow.

"Blow, Boys, Blow" started life as a slaving song, the opening couplet being

A Yankee ship on the Congo River,
Her masts they bend and her sails they shiver.

In this version, the captain is "Holy Joe, the nigger lover," and the mate "a big mulatta come from Antigua." Somewhat later, it was taken over by the "packet-rats" of the Western Ocean, and celebrated the brutalities aboard the Atlantic liners. Doubtless all the well-known masters and mates in that trade have heard themselves picturesquely described in this shanty; but Captain Hayes, who was lost in the *Rainbow* in 1848, is the one whose name seems to have survived.

In other versions, the master is said to be "one-eyed Kelly, the Bowery runner," and the ship is recognized as a Yankee clipper "because the blood runs from her scuppers," or because "they fired a gun, I heard the racket." One couplet dating evidently from Civil War days, inquires:

What do you think she's got for cargo?
Old shot and shell, she breaks the embargo.

Still another tells of her fate:

Her sails were old, her timbers rotten,
His charts the skipper had forgotten.

She sailed away for London city;
Never got there, what a pity!

But the wildest flights of fancy concerned the bill of fare, which was variously stated to consist of "belaying-pin soup and monkey's liver," "mosquito's heart and sandfly's liver," "hot water soup, but slightly thinner," etc. I have never seen in print the *menu* here given; but it is what I heard sung aboard ship in the '90's.

The next shanty celebrates the first and most famous line of American packet-ships to run between New York and Liverpool. Started in 1816, these little ships of 300 to 500 tons furnished for many years the only means of regular communication between this continent and Europe, sailing regularly from New York on the first and sixteenth of each month. In order to keep up their average time of three weeks out and six weeks home, the ships were driven unmercifully, and acquired a bad name among sailors for the iron discipline maintained aboard. The Black Ball Liners carried a crimson swallowtail flag with a black ball in the center, and the same symbol was painted on their fore topsails.

As happened to so many of the old shanties, this one was modernized in later years; and the version given by Terry works a ship from Liverpool to Mobile and brings her back loaded with cotton—a voyage no Blackballer ever made, unless it might have been years later, after the ships ceased to be run as packets.

THE BLACK BALL LINE

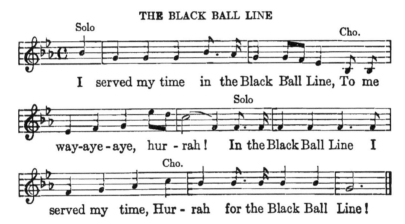

I served my time in the Black Ball Line, To me
way-aye-aye, hur-rah! In the Black Ball Line I
served my time, Hur-rah for the Black Ball Line!

The Black Ball ships they are good and true,
And they are the ships for me and you.

For once there was a Black Ball ship
That fourteen knots an hour could clip.

You will surely find a rich gold mine;
Just take a trip in the Black Ball Line.

Just take a trip to Liverpool,
To Liverpool, that Yankee school.

The Yankee sailors you'll see there,
With red-top boots and short-cut hair.

Probably the most famous of the old packet-ship shanties is "Blow the Man Down." There are at least three distinct "patterns" in the words which have been sung to this old air, which itself, however, seldom varies. (In one version the opening measures bear a striking resemblance to the German folksong "Stille Nacht, Heilige Nacht," but this is probably accidental.) The earliest version again celebrates the Black Ball Line, and the hard lives that were lived aboard those ships. It should be noted that in those days, "blow" meant "knock." The tune will be found on p. 14, with the most recent of the three versions.

1. BLOW THE MAN DOWN

Come, all you young fellows that follow the sea,
To me way—aye, blow the man down!
Now pray pay attention and listen to me.
Give me some time to blow the man down!

I'm a deep water sailor just come from Hongkong;
If you'll give me some whiskey I'll sing you a song.

On a trim Black Ball liner I first served my time,
And in that Black Baller I wasted my prime.

It's when a Black Baller's preparing for sea,
You'd split your sides laughing the sights you would see,

At the tinkers and tailors and sojers and all,
For you'll seldom find sailors aboard a Black Ball.

'Tis when the Black Baller is clear of the land
The crew musters aft at the word of command.

"Lay aft," is the cry, "to the break of the poop,
Or I'll help you along with the toe of my boot."

"Pay attention to orders, now you one and all,
For see, right above you there flies the Black Ball."

'Tis larboard and starboard on deck you will sprawl,
For Kicking Jack Williams* commands that Black Ball.

* Or any skipper whose name happened to occur to the shantyman.

PACKET SHIP ISAAC WEBB, OF NEW-YORK.

"HURRAH FOR THE BLACK BALL LINE!"

Packet Ship Isaac Webb

The second version deals with a case of mistaken identity. Crews of clipper ships like the *Flying Fish* held themselves far superior to the "packet rats" who sailed in the Black Ball Line; and the insult of being mistaken for one of these must have far outweighed the every-day injury of being arrested!

2. Blow the Man Down

As I was a-walking down Paradise Street,
  To me way—aye, blow the man down!
A Liverpool bobby I chanced for to meet,
  Give me some time to blow the man down!

Says he, "You're a Blackballer by the cut of your hair;
I know you're a Blackballer by the clothes that you wear.

"You've sailed in a packet that flies the Black Ball,
You've robbed some poor Dutchman of boots, clothes and all."

"O policeman, policeman, you do me great wrong;
I'm a 'Flying Fish' sailor just home from Hongkong!"

They gave me six months in Liverpool town
For kicking a p'liceman and blowing him down.

Of the Liverpool street which is the scene of this little comedy, Miss C. Fox Smith in her recent book "Sailor Town Days," writes as follows:

"It has had in its day and its way a fame as wide as any street in the world. Its name has been heard on all the winds that blow. It has broken the stately silence of the dawn on still tropic seas. It has mingled with the strong thrumming of the Trades in sail and shroud, and, snatched from the lips of weary, striving, breathless yet still undaunted men, it has added for a moment its puny note to the roar of the stormy Westerlies. It has rung across the loneliest anchorages, the remotest harbors; mat-thatched Malayan villages have heard it, and still, palm-ringed lagoons, and the huddled flat roofs of 'rose-red cities half as old as time.'"

And again,

"Out in the river a big four-master, 'Frisco-bound, is just getting under way. The wind is fair, and already she is hoisting her topsails ready to drop the tug's hawser as soon as she is clear of the anchorage. The mate, a big raw-boned 'blue-nose,' with hands like hammers, and a mouth like a slit across his lean face, is storming about the deck trying to rouse the half-drunk, half-dead crew to some semblance of willing liveliness.

"'Na-ow then—are ye sailors, or ca-arpses, or what are ye? Ain't there a shantyman among the whole blamed crowd o' ye?'

"And, the crew remaining unresponsive, he bursts forth himself in a voice which is strong rather than melodious—accompanying the strains with a sort of obbligato of comments and exhortations, more pointed than polite.

"'As I was a-walking down Paradise Street——

(Give it lip, ye Mahound sojers!)' And in a wavering, half-hearted fashion two or three of the crowd take up the chorus—

'Aye-aye, blow the man down.
A big fat policeman I chanced for to meet—'

('Sing up, there, d—— ye! . . . you, ugly, sing up—air ye deaf or dumb or what are ye?') . . . Great is the power of the shanty over the sailorman! At last the chorus comes roaring out with a will, ringing out across the river, a full-throated volume of sound. . . ."

Of the third, or so-called "shanghai-ing" version, I can not resist the temptation to quote further from Miss Smith's vivid picture:

"A sailor comes rolling down Paradise Street, hands in pockets, head on chest, the very picture of 'spent-up' depression. He is not very drunk, but neither is he quite sober. He has had little to eat, and an old shipmate has just stood him a drink or two, which have gone to his head. Alluring smells are wafted to him from the doors of the public-houses—the 'Dew-drop,' the 'Steer-in,' and the rest—but their charms are not for a poor devil like him, whose pay-roll has long been a thing of the past. Only this morning his boarding-house boss, once so cordial, has looked coldly upon him, and roughly ordered him to make room for a newcomer. It is a case of, in the words of the old sea-song—

In comes old Grouse with a frown,
Saying, 'Get up, Jack, let John sit down.'

John, of course, being the newly-arrived Sou'spainer with a year's pay to burn, and Jack the poor prodigal whose money is spent.

"Even the 'spanking gal' who clings to his arm—a typical Paradise Street charmer—is beginning to waver in her devotion. The *Lightning* is due in port during the next week or two with an old flame of hers on board, and she thinks it is high time Jack 'got a move on.' She has been devoted to him for nearly two months—a long time according to her lights . . . and a whole fortnight since his money was done. If it wasn't for the money, she'd stick to Jack, so she would . . . but there, a poor girl's got to live . . .

"High above the dock sheds rise the slender masts of a clipper ship—the *Donald Mackay, Red Jacket,* or perhaps the mighty *James Baines* herself. Jack stands swaying back on his heels a little unsteadily, and gazes up—up at the fine tracery of her rigging.

"'Ain't she a fine ship?' says Poll artlessly. 'A friend o' mine, she goes with a chap as sails in 'er . . . 'e says they get the best grub 'e ever struck!'

"''Ow'd it be if I was to sign on in 'er, Poll?' says Jack suddenly. 'Glad to get rid o' me, wouldn't yer?'

"Polly sheds a few easy tears.

"'I don't know 'ow hever I'll get on when you're gone, Jack,' she snivels, and her ample bosom heaves readily.

"But Jack only smiles a queer, wry smile. He knows—none better—how much her affection and her tears are really worth. He is sick of the land and its ways—its false friends, its loose women, its pleasures that leave nothing but empty pockets and an aching head. . . .

"And deep down in his muddled mind he knows that stately ship as the symbol of his first love, a love more cruel in her way than this poor Blowsabella of Paradise Street, a love whose gifts are hardship, and cold, and peril in great waters—yet to whom, while breath is in his body, he will continually return.

"'O, Lord love ye, Polly!' he says. 'Ye'll soon get another fancy man!'"

And now, with this long introduction, follows the latest and the best known version of this well-loved old shanty,

BLOW THE MAN DOWN

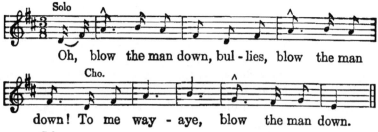

Oh, blow the man down, bul-lies, blow the man

down! To me way - aye, blow the man down.

Oh, blow the man down, bul-lies, blow him right down!

Give me some time to blow the man down!

As I was a-walking down Paradise Street,
A pretty young damsel I chanced for to meet.

She was round in the counter and bluff in the bow,
So I took in all sail and cried "Way enough now."

I hailed her in English, she answered me clear,
"I'm from the Black Arrow bound to the Shakespeare."

So I tailed her my flipper and took her in tow,
And yardarm to yardarm away we did go.

But as we were going she said unto me,
"There's a spanking full-rigger just ready for sea."

That spanking full-rigger to New York was bound;
She was very well manned and very well found.

But soon as that packet was clear of the bar,
The mate knocked me down with the end of a spar,

And as soon as that packet was out on the sea,
'Twas devilish hard treatment of every degree.

So I give you fair warning before we belay;
Don't never take heed of what pretty girls say.

Shanties which were originated by the negro stevedores in the Gulf ports form a large class. The words are for the most part nonsensical, and only the first verse will be given in most of the group that follows; but the tunes are spirited and full of the swing and sense of rhythm which so distinguishes negro folk-music. These songs were developed as an aid to stowing cotton, the bales being rammed tightly into the ship's hold by means of heavy wooden wedges. As the shanties proved useful, either for hauling or for the windlass, they were picked up by the ships' crews and became part of the shantyman's repertoire; but there were numberless others of the same kind, extemporized by negro singers, which did not attain any wide popularity, and of which only traces and allusions here and there remain. Perhaps because their words were even more trivial and meaningless than the general run of shanties, perhaps because their rhythms and cadences were difficult for white sailors to execute, the genuine negro shanties were not esteemed so highly by mixed crews as were those of English and American origin.

JULEY

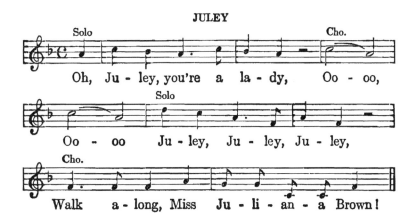

Oh, Ju - ley, you're a la - dy, Oo - oo,
Oo - oo Ju - ley, Ju - ley, Ju - ley,
Walk a - long, Miss Ju - li - an - a Brown!

Sometimes an earlier shanty of non-negro origin was taken by the cotton stevedores and made over into a song to suit themselves. (See "Lowlands," p. 45, and "Clear the Track," p. 43.) "Sing Sally O" (reprinted by permission of Mr. Cecil Sharp) is one of these. Mr. Sharp says it is a variant of "Haul Away Joe."

SING SALLY O

O I say my Mammy Di-nah, What is the mat-ter?

Sing Sal-ly O; Fol-lol-de-day O hur-rah! hur-rah!

My Mam-my Di-nah, Sing Sal-ly O; Fol-lol-de-day.

Another negro shanty, taken with his permission from the collection of Mr. Cecil Sharp, is

LIZA LEE

Li-za Lee, she prom-ised me; Yan-kee John,

Storm-a-long; She prom-ised for to

mar-ry me; Yan-kee John, Storm-a-long.

"Shallo Brown" is another distinctive negro shanty, though its connection with the cotton trade can only be guessed. Captain Robinson says of it:

"I remember hearing it sung by the black crew of an American full-rigged ship, the *Garnet*, of New York, at Macabei, a guano island in the South Pacific. It sounded very musical coming across the still water, while to its accompaniment the captain's gig was pulled up to its place."

The verses which Captain Robinson gives are, however, unusually sentimental for a shanty, and lack the negro flavor.

SHALLO BROWN

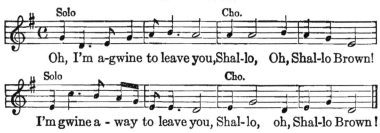

Oh, I'm a-gwine to leave you, Shal-lo,   Oh, Shal-lo Brown!

I'm gwine a - way to leave you, Shal-lo,   oh, Shal-lo Brown!

Come get my clothes in order;
I'm off across the border.

My girl's a bright mulatto;
She hails from Cincinnati.

The packet sails to-morrow,
I'm leaving you to-morrow.

The words, and to some extent the peculiar music, of the following shanty resemble "Shallo Brown"; but I am not positive that it is a negro shanty at all.

GOODBYE, MY LOVE, GOODBYE

I'm bound   a - way   to leave   you,   Good -

bye,   my love, good - bye,   I nev - er   will de -

ceive   you,   Good - bye,   my love, good - bye.

An exception about the popularity of the negro shanties ought to be made in favor of the following, probably the most generally known of the "cotton-drogher" shanties.

ROLL THE COTTON DOWN

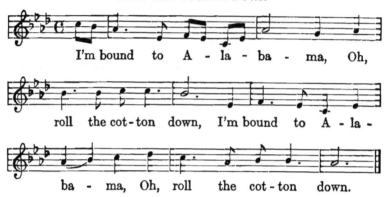

I'm bound to A - la - ba - ma, Oh,
roll the cot-ton down, I'm bound to A - la -
ba - ma, Oh, roll   the cot-ton down.

This shanty was taken over from the colored singers, much in the same way in which they took over "Lowlands" from the whites; and it became the parent of a large family of shanties, some bearing only a remote resemblance to their progenitor. "Lower the Boat Down" is one of these; the words being very likely borrowed from "Rolling King," (p. 39).

> There's only one thing grieves me,
> *Oh, lower the boat down!*
> It's my poor wife and baby,
> *Oh, lower the boat down!*

The following shanty, used on American ships for halliards and sometimes for capstan, was used on British ships in connection with a celebration which was held on board ship when one month at sea. Sailors received one month's pay in advance before leaving port; and of course, duly spent it. After one month at sea, it was considered that this "dead horse" had been worked off, and a rough effigy of canvas and straw remotely resembling a horse, was solemnly carried about the deck as the song was being chanted, and was then hoisted to the yardarm, cut away, and allowed to float off astern. I have never heard of this ceremony taking place aboard an American ship.

The resemblance of the last chorus to "Roll the Cotton Down" is marked, and probably indicates relationship. An anonymous newspaper correspondent states that the "Dead Horse Shanty" was developed from an early negro ballad,

> "Clar de kitchen, old folks, young folks,
> Old Virginny never tire."

POOR OLD MAN

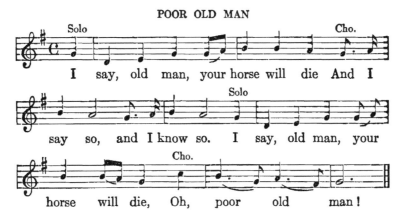

I say, old man, your horse will die And I say so, and I know so. I say, old man, your horse will die, Oh, poor old man!

And if he dies we'll tan his skin, (twice)

And if he lives we'll ride him agin! (twice)

We'll hoist him at the main yardarm, (twice)

And now he's dead we'll bury him deep.   (twice)

The well-known negro shanty, "Run with the Bullgine," is undoubtedly a close relative of "Roll the Cotton Down," but the relationship does not hitherto appear to have been discovered or commented upon.

RUN WITH THE BULLGINE

We'll run all night till the morn - ing, Oh, run with the bull - gine, run! Way, ah - ha, Way, ah - ha! Run with the bull - gine, run!

From the days of the Civil War comes a beautiful and spirited version of "Roll the Cotton Down." The words, of which I have never been able to collect more than a fragment, celebrate the career of the Confederate cruiser *Alabama*.

ALABAMA

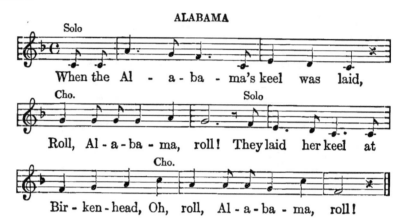

When the Al - a - ba - ma's keel was laid,
Roll, Al - a - ba - ma, roll! They laid her keel at
Bir - ken - head, Oh, roll, Al - a - ba - ma, roll!

Oh, she was built in Birkenhead,
Built in the yard of Jonathan Laird,

Away down the Mersey she rolled one day,
And across the "Western" she ploughed her **way.**

Closely connected with the group of shanties just discussed is another group, consisting of "A Long Time Ago" and its variants. The words of the latter shanty were frequently sung to the tune of "Roll the Cotton Down," but whether the faint but unmistakable resemblance between the two airs is accidental or indicates some relationship, I am unable to say.

A LONG TIME AGO

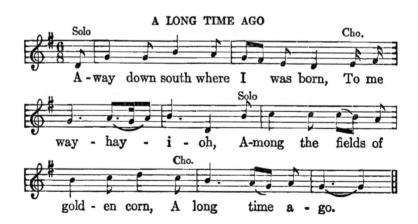

A - way down south where I was born, To me
way - hay - i - oh, A-mong the fields of
gold - en corn, A long time a - go.

I made up my mind to go to sea. (twice)

I wish to God I'd never been born,
To go rambling round and round Cape Horn.

Around Cape Horn where wild winds blow,
Around Cape Horn through sleet and snow.

Around Cape Horn we've got to go,
Around Cape Horn to Callao.

The whalers added another verse:

Around Cape Horn with frozen sails,
Around Cape Horn to fish for whales.

Sometimes, when this was sung as a capstan shanty, a chorus was added to each verse, thus:

A long, long time and a very long time,
To me way—hay—i—oh,
A long long time and a very long time,
A long time ago.

Another version of the words relates that, a long time ago,

A smart Yankee packet lay out in the bay. (twice)

She was waiting a fair wind to get under way. (twice)

If she hasn't a fair wind she's lying there still. (twice)

Sharp prints a version, with the air slightly changed, as follows:

In 'Frisco Bay there lay three ships. (twice)

And one of those ships was old Noah's Ark
All covered over with hickory bark.

They filled up the seams with oakum and pitch. (twice)

And Noah of old commanded this Ark. (twice)

They took two animals of every kind. (twice)

The bull and the cow they started a row.   (twice)

Then said old Noah with a flick of his whip,
Come, stop this row or I'll scuttle the ship.

But the bull put his horns through the side of the Ark,
And the little black dog he started to bark.

So Noah took the dog, put his nose in the hole,
And ever since then the dog's nose has been cold.

This is a good example of the way the shantyman was accustomed to improvise upon an old tune. I venture to guess that some negro shantyman, in a burst of exuberant fancy, sung this version once, in the hearing of the man who sung it to Mr. Sharp. It was certainly not commonly known or sung this way in my seagoing days. Curiously enough, Sharp does not recognize it as a variant of "A Long Time Ago," though he prints the real shanty some ten pages earlier.

Still another variant to "A Long Time Ago," (which may be the original air,) is chiefly remarkable as being the only shanty which can be identified with the Baltimore clippers. It is printed in Sharp's collection under the title "A Hundred Years on the Eastern Shore."

A hundred years on the Eastern Shore,
    O yes, O,
A hundred years on the Eastern Shore,
    A hundred years ago.

Sharp does not print the additional stanzas, which are as follows:

Oh, Bully John from Baltimore,
I knew him well on the Eastern Shore.

Oh, Bully John was the boy for me,
A bucko on land and a bully at sea.

Oh, Bully John, I knew him well,
But now he's dead and gone to hell.

A long, long time and a very long time,
'Tis a very long time since I made this rhyme.

Although the words of the next shanty make it certain that it must have originated on a "down-East" ship, it was not often heard on American vessels. It was well-known in several variants, however, on British ships. Perhaps some idea of the difficulties in the way of the collector of shanties may be gained from the fact that this same shanty appears in the Tozer collection under the name "The Chanty-Man's Song," the first line being "I'm chanty-man of the working party," in Bullen's as "Oh, what did you give for your fine leg of mutton?" and in Terry's as "The Wild Goose Shanty," bringing in the mysterious "Wild Goose Nation" which recurs in several British shanties. All of these versions use practically the same chorus; but none makes mention of the quest for huckleberries.

HUCKLEBERRY HUNTING

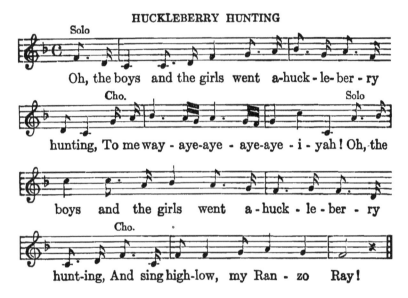

Oh, the boys and the girls went a-huck-le-ber-ry hunting, To me way-aye-aye - aye-aye - i - yah! Oh, the boys and the girls went a-huck-le-ber-ry hunt-ing, And sing high-low, my Ran - zo Ray!

Then a little girl ran off, and a boy he ran after,
And the little girl fell down and he saw her little garter.

He said "I'll be your beau if you'll have me for a feller,"
But the little girl said "No, for my sweetheart's Johnny Miller."

Shanty lore is full of mythical heroes. There is, for example, the doleful ditty of "Reuben Ranzo." This is thought to be originally a whaling song; and the name to have been a corruption of "Lorenzo," a given name common among the Portuguese sailors often found in whaling crews. But there seems little or no evidence to support this theory; and Ranzo has been sung on all classes of merchant ships time out of mind.

REUBEN RANZO

Oh, pi - ty poor Reu - ben Ran - zo, Ran - zo, boys, Ran - zo! Oh, poor old Reu - ben Ran - zo, Ran - zo, boys, Ran - zo!

Oh, Ranzo was no sailor,
So he shipped aboard a whaler.

Oh, Ranzo was no beauty,
He couldn't do his duty.

So they took him to the gangway,
And gave him five-and-thirty.

And that was the end of Ranzo,
Oh, poor old Reuben Ranzo.

There are as many variants in the words and the air of this shanty as there were shantymen to sing it. One version states that the five-and-thirty lashes were applied to poor Reuben "because he was so dirty."

He washed once in a fortnight;
He said it was his birthright.

Another supplies a happy ending, after the episode of the flogging.

Now, the captain being a good man,
He took him to the cabin.

He took him to the cabin,
And gave him wine and brandy.

And he taught him navigation
To fit him for his station.

And he married the captain's daughter,
And still he sails blue water.

And now he's Captain Ranzo,
Hurrah for Captain Ranzo.

Another mythical character is Tommy, the archtype of the wandering sailor.

TOM'S GONE TO HILO

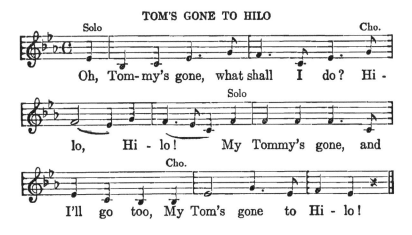

Oh, Tom-my's gone, what shall I do? Hilo, Hi-lo! My Tommy's gone, and
I'll go too, My Tom's gone to Hi-lo!

Oh, Tommy's gone to Liverpool, (twice)
Oh, Tommy's gone to Singapore, (twice)
Oh, Tommy's gone to Boneys Airs,* (twice)

And so on ad lib., the last verse being

My Tommy's gone for ever more. (twice)

It seems fairly certain that "Hilo" is not the Hawaiian port of that name;
for this is a very old shanty, and antedates the use of local Hawaiian place-
names in the sailor's vocabulary. He knew them then as the "Sandwich
Islands," and nothing more. An old sailor told me once that there used to be
a guano port of that name on the West Coast of South America; and later on

* (Buenos Aires).

I found a version of the shanty in print, one line of which was "Hilo town is in Peru." The name was always pronounced "High-low."

In the beginning, the verses were probably sung in couplets:

> Tommy's gone to Liverpool,
> To Liverpool, that Yankee school.

> Tommy's gone to Que-e-bec,
> A-stowing timber on the deck.

> Tommy's gone to Baltimore,
> To dance upon that sanded floor.

> Tommy's gone to Mobile Bay,
> To roll down cotton all the day.

But later shantymen were not so ingenious; and they worked Tommy round the world, to any place they ever heard of that had the right number of syllables, repeating each line to make the verse.

Captain Robinson gives a cynical version, an account of the goings-on of Tom's girl while he was away, and of the quickness with which she was consoled. It concludes philosophically,

> But Tom will get another flame,
> And she will serve him just the same.

The melody is interesting because it seems to show some trace of Oriental influence, the first chorus being reminiscent of Chinese music.

Some versions of "Hanging Johnny," which sketches the career of another nameless hero, attempt to whitewash the character of that reprehensible person by making him say, in the final line, "But I never hanged no*body*."

HANGING JOHNNY

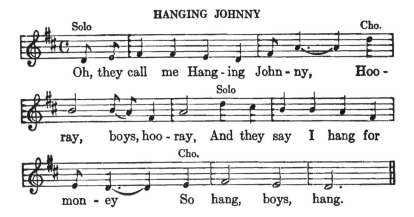

Oh, they call me Hang-ing John-ny, Hoo-ray, boys, hoo-ray, And they say I hang for mon-ey So hang, boys, hang.

First I hung my mother,
Then I hung my brother,

(Other relatives ad lib.)

A rope, a beam, a ladder,
I'll hang you all together.

Masefield says of "Hanging Johnny,"

"It has a melancholy tune that is one of the saddest things I have ever heard. I heard it for the first time off the Horn, in a snowstorm, when we were hoisting topsails after heavy weather. There was a heavy grey sea running, and the decks were awash. The skies were sodden and oily, shutting in the sea about a quarter of a mile away. Some birds were flying about us, screaming.

"I thought at the time that it was the whole scene set to music. I can not repeat those words to their melancholy, wavering music without seeing the line of yellow oilskins, the wet deck, the frozen ropes, and the great grey seas running up into the sky."

A sort of "general utility" shanty, with no particular story, and no lines peculiar to it alone, was "So Handy." These lines and others like them were often drawn upon by the shantyman to "piece out" another shanty when its own lines gave out before the job was done. Miss Laura Smith, in "Music of the Waters," gives a set of words beginning "I'm Handy Jim of Caroline," which tell the story of a sailor who went to court a servant girl, was discovered by her mistress, and went through discomfiting adventures resembling those of

Sir John Falstaff. I have never heard this version, or anything remotely like it, sung at sea.

SO HANDY

Oh, up a - loft this yard must go, So
han-dy, my boys, so han-dy! Oh, up a -loft from
down be - low, So han-dy, my boys, so han - dy!

We'll hoist it high before we go,
And when it's up we'll leave it so.

Oh, sing and haul and haul and sing;
Right up aloft this yard we'll bring.

Stretch her leach and show her clew,
A few more pulls to bring her through.

I thought I heard the first mate say,
"Give one more pull and then belay."

"Cheer'ly Man" is a British shanty; and an early writer in "Harper's Magazine" says it was "frowned upon aboard American ships. . . . No American crew would ever ape the customs prevailing under the flag of an effete monarchy by singing 'Cheer'ly Man.'" This prejudice must have been dissipated by time, because this rousing old shanty was fairly familiar, though never in common use, on American ships in the later days. The words are too racy to reproduce without considerable editing. Captain Robinson gives a version used in catting the anchor, in which the words are all about that somewhat involved process.

CHEER'LY, MAN

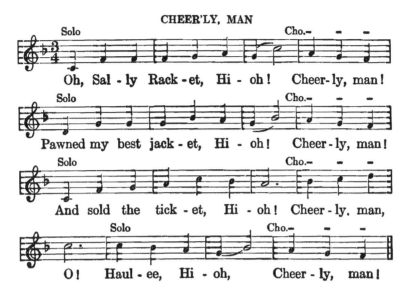

Oh, Sal - ly Rack - et, Hi - oh! Cheer - ly, man!

Pawned my best jack - et, Hi - oh! Cheer - ly, man!

And sold the tick - et, Hi - oh! Cheer - ly, man,

O! Haul - ee, Hi - oh, Cheer - ly, man!

Oh, Nancy Dawson, Hi—oh!
She's got a notion, Hi—oh!
For our old bo'sun, Hi—oh!

Oh, Betsey Baker, Hi—oh!
Lived in Long Acre, Hi—oh!
Married a Quaker, Hi—oh!

Oh, Kitty Carson, Hi—oh!
Jilted the parson, Hi—oh!
Married a mason, Hi—oh!

Avast there, avast, Hi—oh!
Make the fall fast, Hi—oh!
Make it well fast, Hi—oh!

In a class by itself—neither halliard nor capstan shanty—is the so-called "runaway song," in which the crew sang in chorus throughout, tailing on to the rope and running with it down the deck to the stamp and go of the music. It called for a big crew, and so was not much heard on American ships in the later days; but it is one of the few shanties which have crept into song collections ashore.

THE DRUNKEN SAILOR

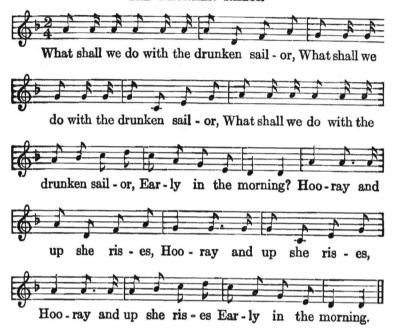

What shall we do with the drunken sail - or, What shall we

do with the drunken sail - or, What shall we do with the

drunken sail - or, Ear - ly in the morning? Hoo - ray and

up she ris - es, Hoo - ray and up she ris - es,

Hoo - ray and up she ris - es Ear - ly in the morning.

Put him in the long-boat and make him bale her.   (thrice)

What shall we do with the drunken soldier (thrice)

Put him in the guardroom till he gets sober.   (thrice)

Musicians have noted with interest the vagaries of this tune. As the notes stand in the text, the air is in D minor. By singing the same notes with two sharps in the signature, the tune is changed to D major; and it was thus sung by some shantymen.* Terry says, "I have generally found that these perversions of the tunes are due to sailors who took to the sea as young men in the last days of the sailing ship, and consequently did not imbibe to the full the old traditions. With the intolerance of youth, they assumed that the model turn given to a shanty by the older sailor was the mark of ignorance, since it did not square with their idea of a major or minor key."

* Whall's version uses these same notes with a natural signature.

III

WINDLASS OR CAPSTAN * SHANTIES

NOT for intermittent operations like pulling and hauling were the songs in this third class used, but for a *continuous process.* In hoisting anchor, warping ship, etc., the rope or cable was wound round the barrel of the capstan, and the men walked steadily round and round it, pushing the capstan bars before them. It follows that any song with a long chorus and a "swing" to it was likely to go well as a capstan shanty. Some of the halliard shanties already given were used in this way; and some of the forecastle songs that follow in the next section. After the Civil War, the marching songs of the Army were great favorites on the forecastle head; and many an anchor came in to the tune of "John Brown's Body" and "Marching Through Georgia." But a number of shanties proper were reserved for this use alone. Of them Masefield says, "The capstan shanties are the most beautiful. . . . In a capstan shanty the solo man begins with his single line of verse. Before he has spoken the last word of it the other men heaving at the bars break out with the first chorus. Immediately before the chorus has come to an end the solo man repeats his line of verse, to be interrupted at the last word by the second chorus, which is generally considerably longer than the first. It is a glorious thing to be on the forecastle-head, heaving at a capstan bar, hearing the chain coming clanking in below you to the music of a noisy shanty sung by a score of sailors."

Though most of the capstan shanties had a chorus sung after the verse and made up of several lines, there were three prime favorites for heaving and hauling which were in the authentic form of the halliard shanty, but which were never used in hoisting sail. The stirring chorus of the first of these three furnishes the title for this book. "Sally Brown" of the many vices and the easy virtue is the heroine of shantydom. Her praises have been sung in all the ports of all the world; but who was the original Sally we know no more than we do of the identity of Johnny Boker and Reuben Ranzo.

* Pronounced ''caps'n.''

SALLY BROWN

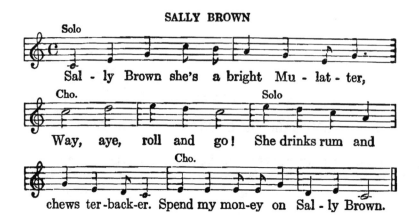

Sal - ly Brown she's a bright Mu - lat - ter,
Way, aye, roll and go! She drinks rum and
chews ter -back-er. Spend my mon-ey on Sal - ly Brown.

Sally Brown, of New York City,
Sally Brown, she is very pretty.

Sally Brown she's a Creole lady;
She's the mother of a nigger baby.

Seven long years I courted Sally,
Seven long years, and she wouldn't marry.

Now my troubles they're all over;
She's married to a nigger soldier.

Another, almost equally a favorite, and known in some one of its endless
variants to every sailing-ship sailor, was

"HEAVE A PAWL!"

The anchor coming in to the tune of a capstan shanty

SHENANDOAH

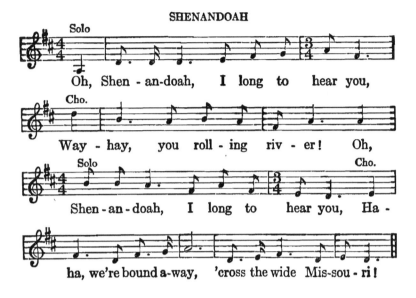

Oh, Shen - an - doah, I long to hear you,

Way - hay, you roll - ing riv - er! Oh,

Shen - an - doah, I long to hear you, Ha -

ha, we're bound a - way, 'cross the wide Mis - sou - ri!

Oh, Shenandoah, I love your daughter, (twice)

Missouri she's a mighty river;
When she rolls down her topsails shiver.

Seven years I courted Sally,
Seven more I longed to have her.

Farewell, my dear, I'm bound to leave you,
Oh, Shenandoah, I'll not deceive you.

This is a late, corrupted form, and was the one used on American ships after the Civil War. The words, as will be seen, are simply nonsense; but it was one of the best known and most frequently used of the capstan shanties. The tune is very free in its rhythms, and can not be written in one *tempo*.

Whall gives the earlier version, which was the story of how a white trader courted the daughter of the famous Indian chieftain Shenandoah, and bore her away in his canoe " 'cross the wide Missouri." He says:

"The seaman of to-day knows nothing of this old song except the tune and one line, 'O Shannadore, I love your daughter.' . . . Originally it was a song, not a shanty, and had nothing to do with salt water. . . . It probably came from the American or Canadian voyageurs, who were great singers. . . ."

The British shantyman's pronunciation is as given by Whall; or even, as Sharp gives it, "Shanadar"; on American ships I have always heard it pronounced "Shanandore."

Few shanties can be as definitely dated as the last of this trio. It must have come into use shortly after our war with Mexico. No one has ever explained why this obscure Mexican general should be as dear to the heart of the sailor as the mighty "Boney" himself; nor why the rôles of Santa Aña and General Taylor should have been exchanged in the shanty. The latter was of course the victor at Monterey, and General Santa Aña fled shortly afterward into exile.

The last whaler to return to New Bedford hauled into dock to the tune of this old shanty; and it was told me by one who was present that the grim old seafarers who gathered on the pierhead to watch, shed tears unashamed as the well-remembered notes rang out across the harbor for the last time.

SANTY ANNA

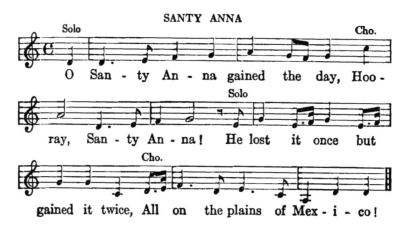

O San - ty An - na gained the day, Hoo-
ray, San - ty An - na! He lost it once but
gained it twice, All on the plains of Mex - i - co!

And Gen'ral Taylor ran away,
He ran away at Monterey.

Oh, Santy Anna fought for fame,
And there's where Santy gained his name.

Oh, Santy Anna fought for gold,
And the deeds he done have oft been told.

And Santy Anna fought for his life,
But he gained his way in the terrible strife.

Oh, Santy Anna's day is o'er,
And Santy Anna will fight no more.

I thought I heard the Old Man say
He'd give us grog this very day.

A favorite "outward-bound" shanty was "Rio Grande." There are few
variations in this fine old tune; but several distinct sets of words. "The
Fishes" (see p. 99) was sometimes sung to this air, as were also the well-
known words of the old ballad, "Where are you going to, my pretty maid?"

However the "Dagos" might pronounce the name, the American sailor dis-
dained any other pronunciation than "Ry-o."

RIO GRANDE

Oh, say, was you ev - er in Ri - o Grande?
Way, you Ri - o! Oh, was you ev - er
on that strand? For we're bound to the Ri - o
Grande! And a - way, you Ri - o! Way, you Ri -
o! Sing fare you well, my pret - ty young
girls, For we're bound to the Ri - o Grande.

Oh, New York town is no place for me;
I'll pack up my bag and go to sea.

Now, you Bowery ladies, we'll let you know
We're bound to the south'ard—O Lord, let her go!

We'll sell our salt cod for molasses and rum,
And get home again 'fore Thanksgiving has come.

Sing good-by to Nellie and good-by to Sue,
And you who are listening, good-by to you.

And good-by, fair ladies we know in this town;
We've left you enough for to buy a silk gown.

Our good ship's a-going out over the bar,
And we'll point her nose for the South-er-on star.

The oldest of the capstan shanties was originally a shore song. (See foreword, p. xviii.) It has always been a great favorite with sailors, and is one of the few shanties which have found their way into modern song collections ashore.

A ROVING

In Am - ster-dam there lived a maid—Mark well what I do say! In Am - ster-dam there lived a maid And she was mis - tress of her trade, And I'll go no more a - rov - ing with you, fair maid! A - rov - ing, a - rov - ing, Since rov-ing's been my ru - i - in, I'll go no more a - rov - ing with you, fair maid!

Her eyes are like two stars so bright, (twice)
Her face is fair, her step is light.

Her cheeks are like the rosebuds red; (twice)
There's wealth of hair upon her head.

Bullen says of the next shanty: "It embodies all the admiration that a sailor used to feel for a great seaman; gives it expression, as it were, though I have never been able to learn who the antitype of Stormalong could have been. I suspect that he was just the embodiment of all the prime seamen the sailor had ever known, and in the song he voiced his heart's admiration."

STORMALONG

Old Storm - y was a fine old man To me way, O storm - a - long! Old Storm - y was a fine old man Way, hay, hay, Mis - ter Storm-a - long!

> Old Stormy he is dead and gone,
> Oh, poor old Stormy's dead and gone.

> We'll dig his grave with a silver spade, (twice)

> And lower him down with a golden chain.   (twice)

> I wish I was old Stormy's son ;
> I'd build me a ship of a thousand ton.

> I'd sail this wide world round and round;
> With plenty of money I'd be found.

> I'd fill her up with New England rum,
> And all my shellbacks they'd have some.

> O Stormy's dead and gone to rest;
> Of all the sailors he was the best.

Old Stormy's obsequies had many variations. Sometimes he was buried at sea:

> He slipped his cable off Cape Horn ;
> Our sails was split and our mainmast gone.

> So we sunk him under a long, long roll, (twice)

Sometimes he was buried

> In Sailor Town up Mobile Bay.

Another version, differing somewhat both in words and tune, was used for pumping:

> Stormalong and round she'll go,
> *To me way, aye, stormalong John!*
> Stormalong through frost and snow,
> *Come along, get along, stormalong John!*

It is possible to make shrewd guesses, which can hardly be more than guesses, however, as to the origin of many of the shanties. "Rolling King," or "South Australia," probably belongs to the days of the British wool-clippers, which ran between London and Melbourne or Sydney.

ROLLING KING

South Aus-tra-lia is my home, Heave a-way, heave a-way! South Aus-tra-lia is my home, I'm bound for South Aus-tra-lia! Heave a-way, heave a-way, Heave a-way, you roll-ing king, I'm bound for South Aus-tra-lia!

There ain't but the one thing grieves my mind,
To leave my wife and child behind.

My wife is standing on the quay;
The tears do start as she waves to me.

Now fare you well and fare you well;
Now fare you well, I wish you well.

"Heave Away," or "We're All Bound to Go," shows little trace of its origin in the form in which its latest seagoing days were spent.

HEAVE AWAY

Some-times we're bound for Liv - er - pool, more
times we're bound for France, Heave a - way, ... my
John - ny, heave a - way   a - way!
Some-times we're bound for Liv - er - pool, more
times we're bound for France, And   a - way,   my
John - ny boy, we're all   bound to   go!

Oh, Johnny, you're a rover, and to-day you sail away.
It's I will be your own sweetheart if you will only stay.

But as it began life along the Liverpool water front, this shanty dealt with the Irish emigration to America in the '50's, most of which passed through that port. Here is one version of the original words:

As I walked out one morning down by the Clarence Dock,
I chanced to hear an Irish girl conversing with Tapscott.

"Oh, good morning, Mister Tapscott," "Good morn, my gal," says he;
"Oh, it's have you got a packet ship for to carry me over the sea?"

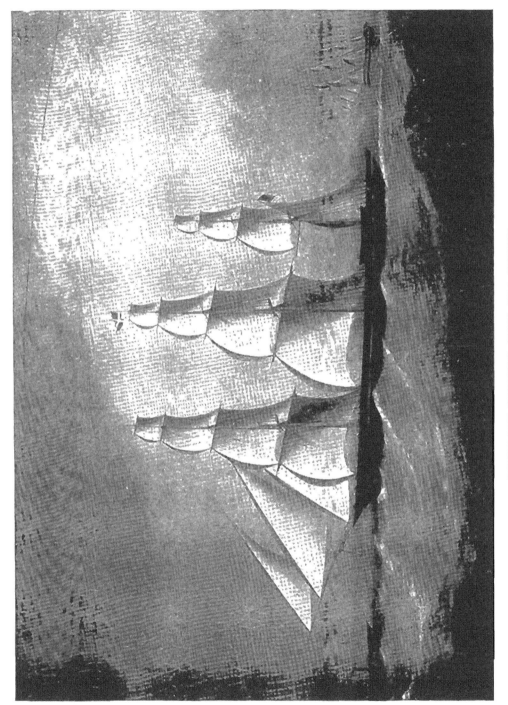

EXTREME CLIPPER SHIP SEA WITCH

Canton to New York in seventy-seven days

"Oh yes, I have a packet ship, a packet of note and fame;
She's lying in the Waterloo Dock, and the *Henry Clay's* her name."

"Bad luck unto the *Henry Clay,* and the day that she set sail,
For them sailors got drunk, broke into me bunk and stole me clothes away.

"It was at Castle Garden they landed me on shore,
And if I marry a Yankee boy, I'll cross the says no more."

William Tapscott was the Liverpool agent for the Black Ball Line, and at one period also for the Red Cross Line of American packets.

In still another version of this song, the words follow the ballad order:

It's of a farmer's daughter so beautiful, I'm told;
Her father died and left her five hundred pounds in gold.

Her uncle and the squire rode out one summer's day;
Young William is in favor, her uncle he did say,
etc.

This version was seldom or never sung on American ships; but its existence hints at the possibility that this shanty was adapted from a folk-ballad brought to sea by some homesick English farmer-boy.

The deep anchorages of the West Coast of South America furnished many a rousing capstan shanty, the long spells of heaving up anchor giving the shantyman incentive and opportunity to create new songs. "Slav Ho" appears to have vanished from the sea with the passing of the guano trade. I have never heard it sung; and copy it from the collection of Captain Robinson. The tune is an imperfect recollection on the part of the shantyman of a German folk-song of the sixteenth century—"Es ritten drei Reiter zum Thore hinaus."

The chorus illustrates another peculiarity of the sailor. He seldom learned more than a few words of a foreign language, and those incorrectly; but he was always vastly amused by the *sound* of an alien, particularly a Latin, tongue, and was given to clumsy paraphrases of it. I recall one unfortunate Spaniard with a many-syllabled name, who was rechristened by his shipmates "Antonio-with-a-Boneo-with-a-Hoo-aw-and-a-Hee-aw-and-a-Compseammo."

SLAV HO!

(Printed by permission of The Bellman, which holds the copyright)

To the Span-ish Main we are bound a-way, Slav

Ho! To the Spanish Main we are bound a-way, Slav

Ho! We're sail-ing a-way in the ear-ly day,

Where the swift bo-ni-tos and dol-phins play! Slav Ho!

Sla-vi-ta, vrai-men-ti-go slee-ga. Slav Ho!

An interesting field for speculation as to its origin is furnished by the next shanty.

CLEAR THE TRACK

Oh, the smart-est clip - per you can find, Ah - hee, ah - ho, are you most done, Is the Marg - 'ret Ev - ans of the Black X Line, So clear a - way the track, let the Bull - gine run! To my hey-rig-a-jig in a low-back car Ah-hee, ah - ho, are you most done With Li - za Lee all on my knee, So clear a - way the track, let the Bull - gine run!

Whall derives this song from a negro minstrel ditty with the chorus:

Walkee up, O walkee up, O walkee up, O way!
Walk into de parlor for to hear de banjo play!

Sharp says that the air is a variant of the Irish folk-song "Shule Agra" and the "low-back car" would support this origin. The probability is that some Irish sailor, ashore on liberty in Mobile, sang "Shule Agra" in a water-front saloon. It pleased the ear of the negroes hanging about outside; and the next day they sang what they could remember while screwing home the great bales of cotton in some Liverpool ship's hold. Negro fashion, they put in the rattling succession of sixteenth notes, and added the "bullgine" for good measure. The crew of the ship heard and liked it, perhaps without recognizing its origin; and took it back with them to Liverpool. There the crew of the *Margaret Evans,* a well-known American packet-ship, lying in the Clarence or the Waterloo Dock, picked it up and fitted in the name of their ship, and took it back to New York, with Liza Lee and the bullgine still in close conjunction with the low-back car, to the puzzlement of future folk-lorists!

"Lowlands" is another well-known shanty which passed through a similar change. The first shanty version is based upon a still earlier English or Scottish ballad which is given by Masefield in "A Sailor's Garland." (It has no con-nection with the better-known ballad of the "Golden Vanity," for which see p. 79.)

I. LOWLANDS

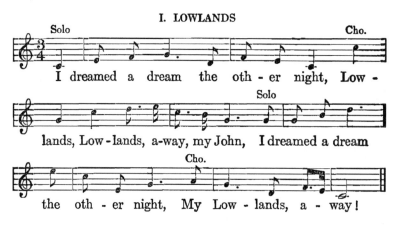

I dreamed I saw my own true love, (twice)

She came to me all in my sleep, (twice)

And then I knew my love was dead. (twice)

And this is what "Lowlands" developed into after it had been adopted by the negro shanty-singers of Mobile.

II. LOWLANDS

Low-lands, low - lands, A - way, my John We're bound away to Mo-bile Bay, My dollar and a half a day Oh, was you ev - er in Mo-bile Bay, Lowlands, low - lands, A - way, my John, A-screwing cot - ton by the day, My dol-lar and a half a day.

* Subsequent verses begin here.

A dollar and a half is a nigger's pay,
A dollar a day is a white man's pay.

The white man's pay is rather high,
The nigger's pay is rather low.

Oh, my old mother she wrote to me,
She wrote to me to come home from sea.

There can be no doubt of the negro origin of the next shanty;* as to how, when or where there is no trace. The lines are a mixture taken from a number of other shanties; scarcely one is peculiar to this shanty alone, although the melody is distinctive enough. Bullen says that it "brings to my mind most

*(Printed by permission from "The Shanty Book," by Richard Runciman Terry.)

vividly a dewy morning in Garden Reach where we lay just off the King of Oudh's palace waiting our permit to moor. I was before the mast in one of Bates' ships, the *Herat,* and when the order came at dawn to man the windlass I raised this shanty and my shipmates sang the chorus as I never heard it sung before or since. There was a big ship called the *Martin Scott* lying inshore of us and her crew were all gathered on deck at their coffee when the order came to ''Vast heaving,' the cable was short. And that listening crew, as soon as we ceased singing, gave us a stentorian cheer, an unprecedented honor. I have never heard that noble shanty sung since, but sometimes even now I can in fancy hear its mellow notes reverberating amid the fantastic buildings of the palace and see the great flocks of pigeons rising and falling as the strange sounds disturbed them."

JOHNNY COME DOWN TO HILO

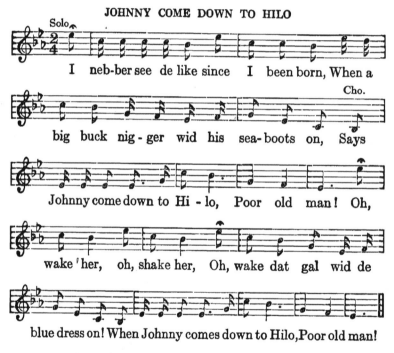

I neb-ber see de like since I been born, When a big buck nig-ger wid his sea-boots on, Says Johnny come down to Hi-lo, Poor old man! Oh, wake 'her, oh, shake her, Oh, wake dat gal wid de blue dress on! When Johnny comes down to Hilo, Poor old man!

I lub a little gal across de sea;
She's a 'Badian beauty, and she says to me:

Oh, was you ebber down in Mobile Bay,
Where dey screws cotton on a summer day?

Did you ebber see de old plantation boss,
And de long-tailed filly and de big black hoss?

The following shanty from Captain Robinson's collection * is purely negro in form, but some of the verbs and the phrase "just gone dead" lead me to suspect that it may be of West Indian origin. Captain Robinson says:

"I heard it during the Civil War at Nassau, while the crew was loading cotton on the ship *Hilja.* . . . Probably it started without any nautical quality, and was adapted for such use by reason of its vigor and swing."

JOHN CHEROKEE

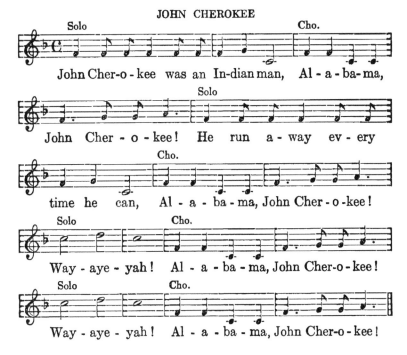

John Cher-o-kee was an In-dian man, Al - a - ba - ma,

John Cher - o - kee! He run a - way ev - ery

time he can, Al - a - ba - ma, John Cher - o -kee!

Way - aye - yah! Al - a - ba - ma, John Cher-o-kee!

Way - aye - yah! Al - a - ba - ma, John Cher-o-kee!

They put him aboard a Yankee ship,
Again he gave the boss the slip.

They catch him again and chain him tight,
And starve him many days and nights.

He have nothing to drink and nothing to eat,
So he just gone dead at the boss's feet.

So they bury him by the old gate post,
And the day he died, you can see his ghost.

* By permission of "The Bellman," which holds the copyright.

Another negro shanty which has no connection with the cotton trade is "The Hog Eye Man," which dates from the days of the " 'forty-niners" in California. It shares with "Abel Brown" the doubtful distinction of being the most indecent of them all. None of its versions can be printed in anything like their entirety. Whall derives the name from a type of barge used on the California coast called "hog-eye"; Terry hints at hidden obscenity in the name itself; but if this were the case, the originators have taken their knowledge with them.

THE HOG EYE MAN

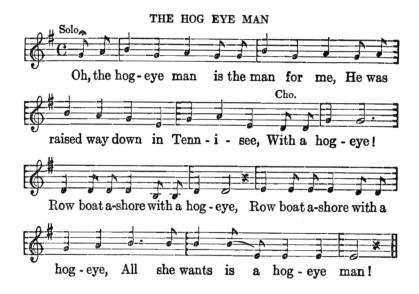

Oh, the hog-eye man   is the man for me, He was
raised way down in Tenn - i - see, With a hog - eye!
Row boat a-shore with a hog - eye, Row boat a-shore with a
hog - eye, All   she wants is   a hog - eye man!

Oh, the hog-eye man is all the go
When he comes down to San Fran-cis-*co*.

Oh, go fetch me down my riding cane,
For I'm going to see my darling Jane.

Oh, who been here since I been gone?
Some big buck nigger wid his sea-boots on.

Oh, I won't wed a nigger, I'll be damned if I do,
He's got jiggers in his feet and he can't wear a shoe.

Another "gold-rush" shanty is

SACRAMENTO

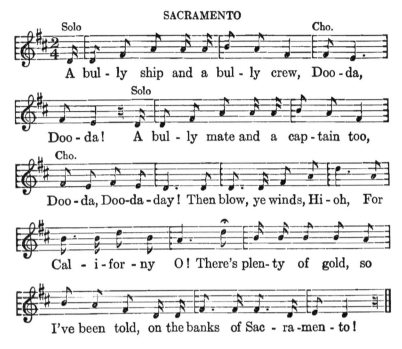

A bul - ly ship and a bul - ly crew, Doo - da,
Doo - da! A bul - ly mate and a cap - tain too,
Doo - da, Doo-da - day! Then blow, ye winds, Hi - oh, For
Cal - i - for - ny O! There's plen - ty of gold, so
I've been told, on the banks of Sac - ra -men - to!

Round Cape Horn in the month of May, (twice)

We came to a land where the cocktail flows, (twice)

Came to a river and I couldn't get across,
Jumped on a nigger and I thought he was a hoss.

This is, of course, the well-known "nigger minstrel" song "Camptown Races." As the words of the latter song were sometimes used at sea, they are given here:

Camptown ladies, sing dis song,
Doo da, Doo da!
Camptown race track five **miles long,**
Doo da, doo da day!

Cho. *Gwine to run all night,*
Gwine to run all day,
I'll bet my money on de bob-tailed nag,
Somebody bet on de bay!

Go down dar wid my hat caved in,
Come back home wid my pockets full ob tin.

De long-tailed filly and de big black hoss
Dey fly de track and dey both cut across,

De blind hoss stickin' in a big mud hole,
Can't touch bottom wid a ten-foot pole.

Old muley cow come out on de track,
De bob he fling her ober his back,

Den fly along like a railroad car
Runnin' a race wid a shootin'-star.

De sorrel hoss he's got a cough,
An' his rider's drunk in de old hay-lof'.

Dar's fo'teen hosses in dis race,
I'm snug in de saddle an' got a good brace.

De bob-tail hoss she can't be beat,
Runnin' around in a two-mile heat.

I win my money on de bob-tail nag,
An' carry it home in de old tow-bag.

Speaking of these two songs, Miss C. Fox Smith says, "as a matter of fact, it is a question which of the two is the older. 'The Banks of Sacramento' certainly dates from the late 'forties or early 'fifties; whether 'Camptown Races' came earlier than that I can not say, but I should doubt it."

According to his biographer, Stephen Foster wrote "Camptown Races" in 1850. There is a chance, but only a bare chance, that he may have picked up the tune from some sailor on the New York water-front; though on the whole it seems to me more probable that after its publication and sudden popularity ashore, it was taken to sea and fitted to new words.

An even more interesting history has the next shanty. It dates from the time of the great Irish emigration to America, and in the form in which it was most popular at sea, was undoubtedly taken over bodily from the music-halls.

PADDY WORKS ON THE RAILWAY

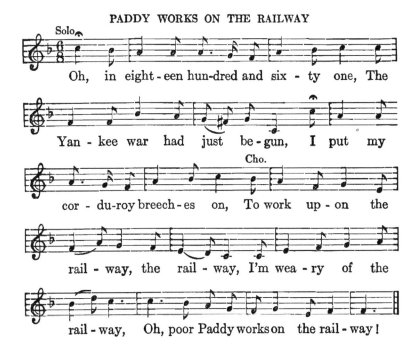

Oh, in eight-een hun-dred and six-ty one, The
Yan - kee war had just be-gun, I put my
cor - du-roy breech-es on, To work up-on the
rail - way, the rail - way, I'm wea - ry of the
rail - way, Oh, poor Paddy works on the rail - way!

Oh, in eighteen hundred and sixty-two,
My corduroy breeches they were new;
I took my pick with a navvy's crew,
    To work upon the railway.

Oh, in eighteen hundred and sixty-three,
I sailed away beyond the sea;
I sailed away to Amerikee,
    To work upon the railway.

Oh, in eighteen hundred and sixty-four,
I landed on the American shore;
I had a pickaxe and nothing more,
    To work upon the railway.
            Etc.

But Terry states that there was an earlier shanty, from which the music-hall song itself had been borrowed, the first verse being as follows:

> When I was a little tiny boy,
> I went to sea in Stormy's employ,
> I sailed away across the sea
> When I was just a shaver.
> It's I was weary of the sea
> When I was just a shaver.

He vouches for the antiquity of this earlier form; and says that his great-uncle used to sing it.

There seems to be no doubt, however, that the next shanty did actually come from a shore ballad. The words are of sailor composition, but the tune is "Larry Doolan."

CAN'T YOU DANCE THE POLKA?

To Tiffany's I took her;
I did not mind expense.
I bought her two gold earrings,
They cost me fifteen cents.

She said, "If you're a sailor,
   Now take me home you may,"
But when I reached her cottage door
   She unto me did say:

"My young man he's a sailor,
   With his hair cut short behind;
My young man he's a sailor,
   And he sails in the Black Ball line."

The reference to "hair cut short behind" places this song toward the last of the packet-ship days, when American sailors had begun to cut their hair in modern fashion, while the British tar still clung to his pig-tail.

"O You Santy" goes to practically the same tune. The words are:

As I was lumbering down the streets of bully London town,
I spied a Yankee clipper ship, to New York she was bound;

And hurrah, you Santy,
My dear honey—
Hurrah, you Santy,
I love you for your money.

Most capstan shanties are "outward-bounders"; but the finest of all was a "homeward-bound shanty." Terry says of it, "This is one of the best beloved of shanties. So strongly did its sentiment appeal to sailors that one never heard the shantyman extemporize a coarse verse to it." And Miss C. Fox Smith sings of it:

There be many good songs we have knocked round the world to,
Manned capstan and halliard, reefed, shifted and furled to,
All round the oceans, since first we did roll
By the Straits of Le Mair for Coquimbo with coal.

All round the world, lad, to ports without number,
Chile for nitrates, the Fraser for lumber,
Where charters might offer or cargoes might call,—
But the homeward-bound shanty's the best of them all.

Slowly GOOD-BYE, FARE YOU WELL!

O fare you well, we're home-ward bound; Good-

bye, fare you well, Good-bye, fare you well!

We're home-ward bound for New York town,

Hur-rah, my boys, we're home-ward bound!

We're homeward bound, heave up and down,
Oh, heave on the capstan and make it spin round.

Our anchors we'll weigh and our sails we will set;
The friends we are leaving we leave with regret.

Oh, heave with a will and heave long and strong,
And sing a good chorus, for 'tis a good song.

We're homeward bound, you've heard them **say,**
Then hook on the catfall and run her away.

She's a flash clipper packet and bound for to go;
With the girls on the towrope she can not say no.

We're homeward bound, and the winds they blow **fair,**
And there'll be many true friends to greet us there.

When the East Indiaman was ready to sail for home, her crew would **add**
a verse:

We're homeward bound across yon sea;
We're homeward bound with Chinee tea.

And the whaleman, when the hold was full of oil and bone, and the course set for New Bedford or Nantucket, sang:

The *whales* we are leaving, we leave with regret!

Another good homeward-bounder was "One More Day." Its origin is uncertain, but it is probably a negro shanty.

ONE MORE DAY

Oh, have you heard the news, my John-ny? One more day! We're home-ward bound to-mor - row, One more day! On - ly one more day, my John-ny, One more day! Oh, rock and row me o - ver, One more day!

We're homeward bound to-morrow, Johnny,
We leave you without sorrow.

Can't you hear the old man snarling, Johnny?
Can't you hear the capstan pawling?

Oh, heave and sight the anchor, Johnny,
Oh, heave and sight the anchor.

I'm bound away to leave you, Johnny,
But I will not deceive you.

Another continuous operation requiring shanties was pumping ship. (In some ships it was more continuous than in others!) In earlier days, the pump handles, or brakes, worked up and down; but later wheel pumps were introduced, with the brakes attached to the rims. Pumping ship was likely to be a long, monotonous spell of hard work, unless enlivened by a song. Almost any of the capstan shanties could be used on the pump-brakes, but a few were kept, by the force of convention, for no other use, as in the next example. Jack would have his joke, even about that most dreaded of dangers, fire at sea; and the joke lay in his choosing non-inflammable portions of the ship in which to locate his imaginary fire. There is always, of course, a fire in the galley, which is the ship's kitchen.

FIRE DOWN BELOW

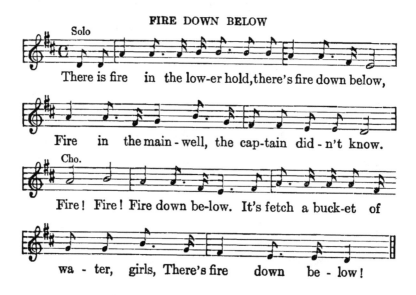

There is fire in the low-er hold, there's fire down below,
Fire in the main-well, the cap-tain did-n't know.
Fire! Fire! Fire down be-low. It's fetch a buck-et of
wa - ter, girls, There's fire down be - low!

There is fire in the fore-top, fire in the main,
Fire in the windlass and fire in the chain.

There is fire in the fore-peak, fire down below,
Fire in the chain-plates, the bo'sun didn't know.

There is fire up aloft, there's fire down below,
Fire in the galley, the cook he didn't know.

The negro shantyman contributed the following—which could have been used for ordinary capstan work by substituting the word "heave" for "pump."

MOBILE BAY

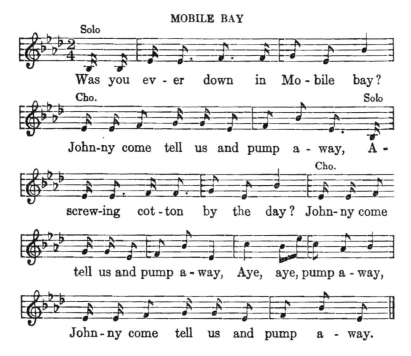

Was you ev - er down in Mo - bile bay? John-ny come tell us and pump a - way, A - screw-ing cot - ton by the day? John- ny come tell us and pump a - way, Aye, aye, pump a - way, John - ny come tell us and pump a - way.

We close our collection of capstan shanties, appropriately, with the one which was always the last to be sung when the voyage was over. Its origins go back to the Atlantic packet ship shanties again, for it was originally one of the oldest of these, "Across the Western Ocean."

ACROSS THE WESTERN OCEAN

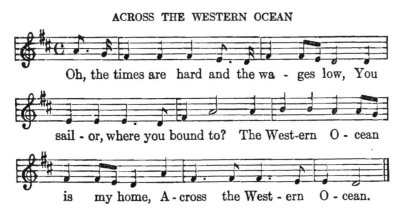

Oh, the times are hard and the wa - ges low, You sail - or, where you bound to? The West-ern O - cean is my home, A-cross the West - ern O - cean.

We are going away from friends and home,
We are going away to search for gold.

Fathers and mothers, say good-by,
Sisters and brothers, don't you cry.

The modern version, variously known as "Leave Her, Johnny," or "Time for Us to Leave Her," is reserved for the last task after the ship is fast to the pier, and the crew are about to go ashore—the last spell at the pumps. It is the sailor's farewell song, in which he expresses without fear—since the voyage is over—his opinion of ship and officers. The newspapers not long ago carried a story of how the striking firemen on a transatlantic liner marched ashore in New York singing this old song. It shows the extraordinary persistence of the shanty, that it should still be known and sung in the stokeholds of steamers!

LEAVE HER, JOHNNY

I thought I heard the Old Man say,

Leave her, John-ny, leave her! You can go a-shore and

draw your pay, It's time for us to leave her!

You may make her fast and pack your gear,
And leave her moored to the West Street pier.

The winds were foul, the work was hard,
From Liverpool docks to the Brooklyn yard.

She would neither steer nor wear nor stay,
She shipped it green both night and day.

She shipped it green and she made us curse,—
The mate is a devil and the old man worse.

The winds were foul, the ship was slow,
The grub was bad, the wages low,

The winds were foul, the trip was long,
But before we go we'll sing this song.

We'll sing, oh, may we never be
On a hungry bitch the like of she.

Another version:

Oh, the times are hard and the wages low;
I'll pack my bag and go below.

It's growl you may, but go you must;
It matters not whether you're last or fust.

I'm getting thin and growing sad
Since first I joined this wooden-clad.

I thought I heard the second mate say:
"Just one more drag and then belay."

(Pumping version, sometimes used when at sea.)

A dollar a day is a sailor's pay,
To pump all night and work all day.

The times are hard and the ship is old,
And there's six feet of water in her hold.

The bo'sun shouts, the pumps stand by,
But we can never suck her dry.

Oh, heave around the pump-bowls bright;
There'll be no sleep for us this night.

Heave around, or we shall drown;
Don't you feel her settling down?

The rats have gone, and we the crew,
It's time, by God, that we went too.

IV

FORECASTLE SONGS *

WHEN the day's work was over, supper eaten and the mess-kits put away, and pipes or cheeks, as the case might be, filled with strong plug tobacco, came the sailor's time of leisure. During the "dog-watch," in the early evening, both watches were on deck, gathered about the main hatch in pleasant weather, or stowed away in sheltered spots when it was inclement. Singing, dancing and yarn-spinning were then the order of the day; cherished instruments were brought out, perhaps a squeaky fiddle, or an accordion, beloved of the sailor and hated, for some unknown reason, by every master mariner I ever knew. Happy the "crowd" that had a "nigger singer," for he had a repertoire all his own. Songs popular ashore had their place in these evening concerts, of course—sentimental songs for choice—but never the sailor songs so favored by amateurs ashore. I never heard such a song as "A Wet Sheet and a Flowing Sea" or "Ben Backstay" sung by sailors; they are made supremely uncomfortable by hearing others sing them. The songs of all lands had their part in these musical evenings, and many old English ballads were treasured in the sailor's memory, but I am including here only such as are part of the common heritage of England and America; or as seem from their wording to have originated on American ships. I hesitated long over that beautiful old song "Farewell and Adieu to You, Spanish Ladies," in which the ship is worked up Channel to the Downs, picking up light after light; and that more modern but equally beautiful homeward-bound song,

> Rolling home, rolling home,
> Rolling home across the sea,
> Rolling home to Merry England,
> Rolling home, dear land, to thee!

But I finally decided to take no advantage of the fact that they were sung, and frequently sung, aboard our ships, but to exclude them as being British property.

The last place in which certain patriotic ballads of early American history

---

* In the British merchant service, these songs were known as "fore-bitters."

were sung, was probably in the forecastle of American ships; and they were current there long after they had been forgotten ashore. The most stirring of these goes by various names; "The Ranger" (although the real air called by that name is quite different from the one to which sailors sang the words), "The Yankee Man-of-War," or the name under which my father used to sing it, "The Stately Southerner." It recounts an exploit of John Paul Jones off the Irish coast in his privateer, the *Ranger,* which was fitted out in Portsmouth, N. H., in 1777. As she had no connection with the South that I have been able to discover, I am unable to state why she appears in the song as "The Stately Southerner."

THE STATELY SOUTHERNER

It was the State - ly South - er - ner, that car-ried the Stripes and Stars, The whist-ling wind from west - nor'-west blew thru her pitch-pine spars, With her star-board tacks a - board, my boys, she hung up to the gale,—'Twas an au - tumn night, we raised the light on the Old Head of Kin - sale.

It was a clear and cloudless night; the wind blew steady and strong,
As gaily over the sparkling deep our good ship bowled along.
With the fiery foam beneath her bows the white wave she did spread,
And bending alow her bosom in snow she buried her lee cathead.

There was no talk of short'ning sail by him who walked the poop,
And 'neath the press of her ponderous jib the boom bent like a hoop;
And the groaning waterways told the strain that held her stout main-tack,
But he only laughed as he gazed abaft at the white and glist'ning track.

The mid-tide meets in the channel waves that flow from shore to shore,
And the mist hung heavy along the land from Featherstone to Dunmore,
And that sterling light on Tuskar Rock, where the old bell tolls each hour,
And the beacon light that shone so bright was quenched on Waterford tower.

What looms upon our starboard bow, what hangs upon the breeze?
'Tis time our good ship hauled her wind abreast the old Saltees,
For by her ponderous press of sail and by her stunted spars
We saw that our morning visitor was a British man-o'-war.

Up spake our noble Captain then as a shot ahead of us passed:
"Haul snug your flowing courses! Lay your topsails to the mast!"
Those Englishmen gave three loud hurrahs from the deck of their covered ark,
And we answered back by a solid broadside from the deck of our patriot bark.

"Out booms! Out booms!" our skipper cried: "Out booms and give her sheet!"
For the swiftest keel that ever was launched in all of the British fleet
Came pondering down upon us with the white foam at her bow;
"Out booms! Out booms! and give her sheet! spare not your canvas now!"

But a swifter keel was 'neath our feet, nor did our sea-boys dread
When the Star-spangled banner was hoisted; to the mizzen peak was spread,
And amid a thundering shower of shot with stunsails hoisting away,
Down the North Channel Paul Jones did steer just at the break of day.

The next furnishes a sea-history—from the American point of view—of the War of 1812. It was good for a fight any time there happened to be a Britisher in the forecastle!

YE PARLIAMENT OF ENGLAND

Ye Par - lia - ment of Eng - land, ye
Lords and Com-mons too, Con - sid - er well what
you're a - bout, what you're a - bout to do,
For you're to war with Yan - kees, and I'm
sure you'll rue the day You roused the Sons of
Lib - er - ty in North A - mer - i - ca!

You first confined our commerce,
    And said our ships shan't trade,
You next impressed our seamen,
    And used them as your slaves;
You then insulted Rodgers,
    While ploughing o'er the main,
And had we not declarèd war,
    You'd have done it o'er again.

You tho't our frigates were but few,
    And Yankees could not fight,
Until brave Hull your *Guerrière* took,
    And banished her from your sight.

The *Wasp* then took your *Frolic,*
   We'll nothing say to that,
The *Poictiers* being of the line
   Of course she took her back.

The next, your *Macedonian,*
   No finer ship could swim,
Decatur took her gilt work off,
   And then he sent her in.
The *Java,* by a Yankee ship
   Was sunk you all must know;
The *Peacock* fine, in all her plume,
   By Lawrence down did go.

Then, next you sent your *Boxer,*
   To box us all about,
But we had an *Enterprising* brig
   That boxed your *Boxer* out;
She boxed her up to Portland,
   And moored her off the town,
To show the sons of liberty
   The *Boxer* of renown.

The next upon Lake Erie,
   Where Perry had some fun,
You own he beat your naval force,
   And caused them for to run;
This was to you a sore defeat,
   The like ne'er known before—
Your British squadron beat complete—
   Some took, some run ashore.

There's Rodgers, in the *President,*
   Will burn, sink, and destroy;
The *Congress,* on the Brazil coast,
   Your commerce will annoy;
The *Essex,* in the South Seas,
   Will put out all your lights,
The flag she waves at her mast-head—
   "Free Trade and Sailors' Rights."

This spirited account of the taking of the *Guerrière* by the U. S. frigate *Constitution* went to the tune of "The Pretty Lass of Derby O!" After the defeat of the *Chesapeake* by the *Shannon,* the British imitated the song here given by one celebrating their own victory.

THE CONSTITUTION AND GUERRIÈRE

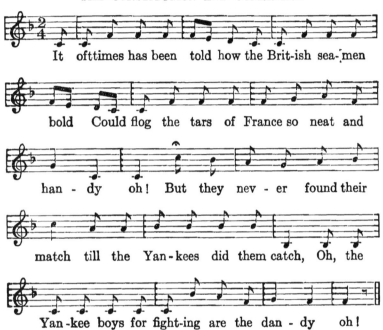

It ofttimes has been told how the Brit-ish sea-men bold Could flog the tars of France so neat and han - dy oh! But they nev - er found their match till the Yan - kees did them catch, Oh, the Yan - kee boys for fight-ing are the dan - dy oh!

The *Guerrière* so bold,
On the foaming ocean rolled,
Commanded by proud Dacres the grandee, oh!
With as choice a British crew
As a rammer ever drew,
Could flog the Frenchmen two to one so handy, oh!

When this frigate hove in view,
Says proud Dacres to his crew,
"Come, clear ship for action and be handy, oh!
On the weather gage, boys, get her,"
And to make his men fight better,
He gave to them gunpowder mixed with brandy, oh!

Then Dacres loudly cries,
  "Make this Yankee ship your prize,
You can in thirty minutes, neat and handy, oh!
  Twenty-five's enough I'm sure,
  And if you'll do it in a score,
I'll treat you to a double share of brandy, oh!"

The British shot flew hot,
  Which the Yankees answered not,
Till they got within the distance they called handy, oh!
  "Now," says Hull unto his crew,
  "Boys, let's see what we can do,
If we take this boasting Briton we're the dandy, oh!"

The first broadside we poured
  Took her mainmast by the board,
Which made this lofty frigate look abandon'd, oh!
  Then Dacres shook his head;
  To his officers he said,
"Lord! I didn't think those Yankees were so handy, oh!"

Our second told so well
  That their fore and mizzen fell
Which dous'd the royal ensign neat and handy, oh!
  "By George!" says he, "we're done,"
  And they fired a lee gun,
While the Yankees struck up Yankee doodle dandy, oh!

Then Dacres came on board
  To deliver up his sword,
Which he was loath to lose, it was so handy, oh!
  "Oh, keep your sword," says Hull,
  "For it only makes you dull;
Cheer up and let us have a little brandy, oh!"

Now, fill your glasses full,
  And we'll drink to Captain Hull,
And merrily we'll push about the brandy, oh!
  John Bull may boast his fill,
  But let the world say what it will,
The Yankee boys for fighting are the dandy, oh!

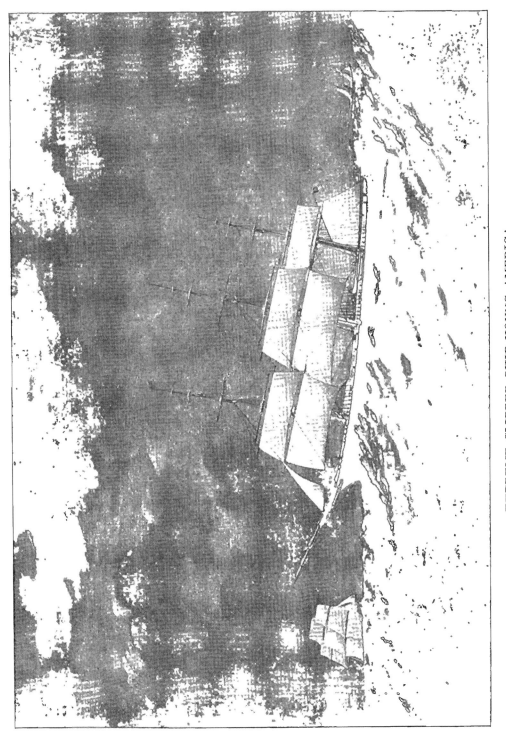

EXTREME CLIPPER SHIP YOUNG AMERICA

San Francisco to New York in eighty-three days

A favorite song of the old navy follows. The *Jamestown* was a sloop-of-war, built in 1844, and not to be confused with the Confederate gunboat of the same name. Her only claim to renown is that she was the relief ship sent by the United States government to Ireland to succor the victims of the famine of 1847. The song tells of a cruise "up the Straits," as sailors used to call Mediterranean waters.

THE *JAMESTOWN* HOMEWARD BOUND

The farm-er's heart with joy is filled when his crops are good and sound, But who can feel the wild de-light of the sai-lor home-ward bound? For three long years have passed a-way since we left free-dom's shore, Our long-felt wish has come at last, and we're homeward bound once more.

Chorus (tune same as last two lines of verse, repeated).

To where the sky is as clear as the maiden's eye who longs for our return,
To the land where milk and honey flows and liberty it was born.
So fill our sails with the favoring gales, and with shipmates all around
We'll give three cheers for our Starry flag and the "Jamestown" homeward bound.

To the Mediterranean shores we've been, and its beauties we have seen,
And Sicily's grand and lofty hills and Italy's gardens green,
, We've gazed on Mount Vesuvius, with its rugged slumbering dome;
Night is the time in that red clime when the sailor thinks of home.

We've strayed round Pompeii's ruined walls, and on them carved our names,
And thought of its ancient beauties past and vanished lordly dames,
And gazed on tombs of mighty kings who oft in battle won,
But what were they all in their sway with our brave Washington?

And now we have arrived in port and stripping's our last job,
And friendly faces look around in search of Bill or Bob.
They see that we are safe at last from the perils of the sea,
Saying, "You're welcome, Columbia's mariners, to your homes and liberty."

Of old ballads sung in the forecastle there was no end. This is the sea-going version of a very ancient North of England ballad—"The Old Tup." It is taken from Captain Robinson's collection, and reprinted by permission of "The Bellman," which holds the copyright. Many a crew must have been "sold" by the simple trick of that last verse, and realized the sell only when they had to roar out their chorused denial.

DERBY RAM

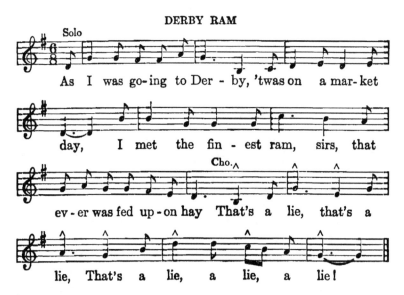

As I was go-ing to Der-by, 'twas on a mar-ket day, I met the fin-est ram, sirs, that ev-er was fed up-on hay That's a lie, that's a lie, That's a lie, a lie, a lie!

This ram and I got drunk, sir, as drunk as drunk could be,
And when we sobered up, sir, we were far away out on the sea.

This wonderful old ram, sir, was playful as a kid;
He swallowed the captain's spyglass along with the bo'sun's fid.

One morning on the poop, sir, before eight bells was rung,
He grabbed the captain's sextant and took a shot at the sun.

One night 'twas wet and rough, sir, and the wind was blowing keen,
He borrowed my suit of oilskins and he took my trick at the wheel.

The butcher who killed this ram, sir, was up to his knees in blood,
And the boy who told the tale, sir, was carried away with the flood.

The crew of the *Vencedora* * are handsome, strong and brave,
The smartest lot of sailors that ever sailed over the wave!

Many a forecastle has resounded to the endless and lugubrious verses of "Captain Kidd" (sung to the tune of "Samuel Hall"). Captain Kidd's real name was, of course, William; but he always appeared as "Robert" in the old song.

CAPTAIN KIDD

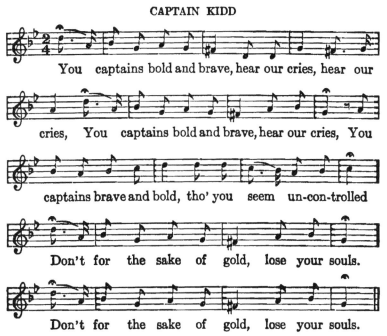

* Or any ship on which the song was being sung.

My name was Robert Kidd, when I sail'd, when I sail'd,
  My name was Robert Kidd, when I sail'd,
My name was Robert Kidd, God's laws I did forbid,
  And so wickedly I did, when I sail'd.

My parents taught me well, when I sail'd, when I sail'd,
  My parents taught me well, when I sail'd,
My parents taught me well, to shun the gates of hell,
  But against them I rebell'd, when I sail'd.

I cursed my father dear, when I sail'd, when I sail'd,
  I cursed my father dear, when I sail'd,
I cursed my father dear, and her that did me bear,
  And so wickedly did swear, when I sail'd.

I made a solemn vow, when I sail'd, when I sail'd,
  I made a solemn vow, when I sail'd,
I made a solemn vow to God I would not bow,
  Nor myself one prayer allow, as I sail'd.

I'd a Bible in my hand, when I sail'd, when I sail'd,
  I'd a Bible in my hand, when I sail'd,
I'd a Bible in my hand by my father's great command,
  And sunk it in the sand, when I sail'd.

I murdered William Moore, as I sail'd, as I sail'd,
  I murdered William Moore, as I sail'd,
I murdered William Moore, and left him in his gore,
  Not many leagues from shore, as I sail'd.

And being cruel still, as I sail'd, as I sail'd,
  And being cruel still, as I sail'd,
And being cruel still, my gunner I did kill,
  And his precious blood did spill, as I sail'd.

My mate was sick and died, as I sail'd, as I sail'd,
  My mate was sick and died, as I sail'd,
My mate was sick and died, which me much terrified,
  When he call'd me to his bedside, as I sail'd.

And unto me he did say, see me die, see me die,
   And unto me did say, see me die,
And unto me did say, take warning now by me,
   There comes a reckoning day, you must die.

You can not then withstand, when you die, when you die,
   You can not then withstand, when you die,
You can not then withstand the judgment of God's hand,
   But bound then in iron bands you must die.

I was sick and nigh to death, as I sail'd, as I sail'd,
   I was sick and nigh to death, as I sail'd,
I was sick and nigh to death, and I vow'd at every breath,
   To walk in wisdom's ways, as I sail'd.

I thought I was undone, as I sail'd, as I sail'd,
   I thought I was undone, as I sail'd,
I thought I was undone and my wicked glass had run,
   But health did soon return, as I sail'd.

My repentance lasted not, as I sail'd, as I sail'd,
   My repentance lasted not, as I sail'd,
My repentance lasted not, my vows I soon forgot,
   Damnation's my just lot, as I sail'd.

I steer'd from sound to sound, as I sail'd, as I sail'd,
   I steer'd from sound to sound, as I sail'd,
I steer'd from sound to sound and many ships I found
   And most of them I burned, as I sail'd.

I spy'd three ships from France, as I sail'd, as I sail'd,
   I spy'd three ships from France, as I sail'd,
I spy'd three ships from France to them I did advance,
   And took them all by chance, as I sail'd.

I spy'd three ships of Spain, as I sail'd, as I sail'd,
   I spy'd three ships of Spain, as I sail'd,
I spy'd three ships of Spain, I fired on them amain,
   Till most of them were slain, as I sail'd.

I'd ninety bars of gold, as I sail'd, as I sail'd,
    I'd ninety bars of gold, as I sail'd,
I'd ninety bars of gold and dollars manifold,
    With riches uncontrolled, as I sail'd.

Then fourteen ships I saw, as I sail'd, as I sail'd,
    Then fourteen ships I saw, as I sail'd,
Then fourteen ships I saw and brave men they were,
    Ah! they were too much for me, as I sail'd.

Thus being o'ertaken at last, I must die, I must die,
    Thus being o'ertaken at last, I must die,
Thus being o'ertaken at last, and into prison cast
    And sentence being passed, I must die.

Farewell the raging main, I must die, I must die,
    Farewell the raging main, I must die,
Farewell the raging main, to Turkey, France, and Spain,
    I ne'er shall see you again, I must die.

To Newgate now I'm cast, and must die, and must die,
    To Newgate now I'm cast, and must die,
To Newgate I am cast, with a sad and heavy heart,
    To receive my just desert, I must die.

To Execution Dock I must go, I must go,
    To Execution Dock I must go,
To Execution Dock will many thousands flock,
    But I must bear the shock, I must die.

Come all you young and old, see me die, see me die,
    Come all you young and old, see me die,
Come all you young and old, you're welcome to my gold,
    For by it I've lost my soul, and must die.

Take warning now by me, for I must die, for I must die,
    Take warning now by me, for I must die,
Take warning now by me, and shun bad company,
    Lest you come to hell with me, for I must die.

    The dark old days of the "Guinea trade" furnish the background for the next song. Slaving, openly carried on by American ships, in the eighteenth century, was prohibited by several acts of Congress between the years 1807 and

1823; and thereafter the smuggling of slaves gradually lessened, though there were convictions of American shipmasters for this crime as late as 1861.

This song probably dates from somewhere between the years 1819 and 1825, when the West Indies were finally cleared of pirates by the joint efforts of the United States and several of the European naval powers. Before this date, according to Spear,* "Pirates swarmed over the West Indian seas, and their doings were justly believed to be, in many cases, chargeable to the slave trade. The slavers turned pirates, and the pirates turned slavers, as occasion warranted."

This was the era when Baltimore stood third of all American ports as a shipping center, but neither the *Flying Cloud* nor Captain Moore have been identified through the literature of the times. The name of the British frigate was imperfectly recalled by the singer, and the ninth and tenth stanzas have probably been interpolated at some later date, but there is no reason to doubt that the song describes actual occurrences.

THE *FLYING CLOUD*

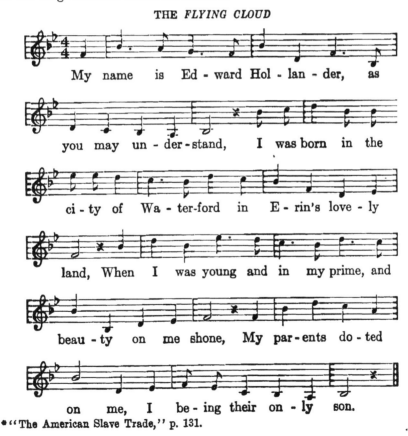

My name is Ed - ward Hol - lan - der, as
you may un - der - stand, I was born in the
ci - ty of Wa - ter-ford in E - rin's love - ly
land, When I was young and in my prime, and
beau - ty on me shone, My par - ents do - ted
on me, I be - ing their on - ly son.

* "The American Slave Trade," p. 131.

My father bound me to a trade in Waterford's fair town,
He bound me to a cooper there, by the name of William Brown.
I served my master faithfully for eighteen months or more,
Till I shipped on board of the *Ocean Queen*, belonging to Tramore.

When we came unto Bermuda's isle, there I met with Captain Moore,
The commander of the *Flying Cloud,** hailing from Baltimore,
He asked me if I'd ship with him, on a slaving voyage to go,
To the burning shores of Africa, where the sugar cane does grow.

It was after some weeks' sailing we arrived off Africa's shore,
And five hundred of these poor slaves, my boys, from their native land we bore.
We made them walk in on a plank, and we stowed them down below;
Scarce eighteen inches to a man was all they had to go.

The plague and fever came on board, swept half of them away;
We dragged their bodies up on deck and hove them in the sea.
It was better for the rest of them if they had died before,
Than to work under brutes of planters in Cuba for ever more.

It was after stormy weather we arrived off Cuba's shore,
And we sold them to the planters there, to be slaves for ever more.
For the rice and the coffee seed to sow beneath the broiling sun,
There to lead a wretched, lonely life till their career was run.

It's now our money is all spent, we must go to sea again,
When Captain Moore he came on deck and said unto us men,
"There is gold and silver to be had if with me you'll remain,
And we'll hoist the pirate flag aloft, and we'll scour the Spanish Main."

We all agreed but three young men who told us them to land,
And two of them was Boston boys, the other from Newfoundland.
I wish to God I'd joined those men and went with them on shore,
Than to lead a wild and reckless life, serving under Captain Moore.

The *Flying Cloud* was a Yankee ship of five hundred tons or more;
She could outsail any clipper ship hailing out of Baltimore.
With her canvas white as the driven snow, and on it there's no specks,
And forty men and fourteen guns she carried on her decks.

* Not to be confused with the California clipper ship *Flying Cloud*, which was not
built until 1851.

It's oft I've seen that gallant ship, with the wind abaft her beam,
With her royals and her stunsails set, a sight for to be seen,
With the curling wave from her clipper bow, a sailor's joy to feel,
And the canvas taut in the whistling breeze, logging fourteen off the reel.

We sank and plundered many a ship down on the Spanish Main,
Caused many a wife and orphan in sorrow to remain;
To them we gave no quarter, but gave them watery graves,
For the saying of our captain was, that dead men tell no tales.

Pursued we were by many a ship, by frigates and liners too,
Till at last a British man-o'-war, the *Dungeness* (?), hove in view.
She fired a shot across our bow, as we sailed before the wind,
Then a chainshot cut our mainmast down, and we fell far behind.

Our crew they beat to quarters as she ranged up alongside,
And soon across our quarter-deck there ran a crimson tide.
We fought till Captain Moore was killed and twenty of our men,
Till a bombshell set our ship on fire, we had to surrender then.

It's next to Newgate we were brought, bound down in iron chains,
For the sinking and the plundering of ships on the Spanish Main.
The judge he found us guilty, we were condemned to die;
Young men, a warning by me take, and shun all piracy.

Then fare you well, old Waterford, and the girl that I adore;
I'll never kiss your cheek again, or squeeze your hand no more.
For whiskey and bad company first made a wretch of me;
Young men, a warning by me take, and shun all piracy.

"Greenland Fishery" or "The Whale" was not more popular on whaling ships than in the ships of the merchant marine. It arose in the British, not the American, whaling trade, probably in the latter part of the eighteenth century, and in the earlier British versions, the ship's name, the *Lion*, and the captain's, Speedicutt, are both preserved.

GREENLAND FISHERY

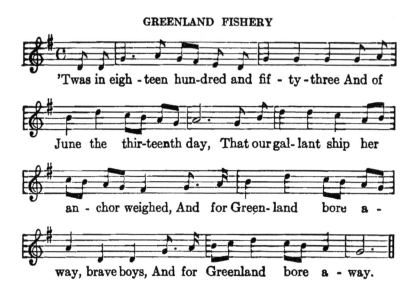

'Twas in eigh - teen hun-dred and fif - ty -three And of June the thir-teenth day, That our gal-lant ship her an - chor weighed, And for Green- land bore a - way, brave boys, And for Greenland bore a - way.

The lookout in the crosstrees stood,
With his spyglass in his hand.
"There's a whale, there's a whale, there's a whalefish," he cried,
"And she blows at every span, brave boys,
And she blows at every span."

The captain stood on the quarterdeck,
And a fine little man was he.
"Overhaul! Overhaul! Let your davit-tackles fall,
And launch your boats for sea, brave boys,
And launch your boats for sea."

Now the boats were launched and the men aboard,
And the whale was in full view;
Resolv-ed was each seaman bold
To steer where the whalefish blew, brave boys,
To steer where the whalefish blew.

We struck that whale, the line paid out,
But she gave a flourish with her tail;
The boat capsized and four men were drowned,
And we never caught that whale, brave boys,
And we never caught that whale.

"To lose the boat," our captain said,
"It grieves my heart full sore;
But oh! to lose four gallant men,
It grieves me ten times more, brave boys,
It grieves me ten times more."

"The winter star doth now appear,
So, boys, we'll anchor weigh;
It's time to leave this cold country,
And homeward bear away, brave boys,
And homeward bear away."

Oh, Greenland is a dreadful place,
A land that's never green,
Where there's ice and snow, and the whalefishes blow,
And the daylight's seldom seen, brave boys,
And the daylight's seldom seen.

The next two are variants, much garbled, of very early English ballads. Readers who are curious about origins can find the original of "High Barbaree" in "The Sea's Anthology," by Patterson, under the title, "The Saylor's Onely Delight: Showing the Brave Fight betweene the *George Aloe* and the *Sweepstake* and certaine *Frenchmen* on the Sea." (The version here given was collected by Mr. George H. Taber in New Bedford, and is printed with his permission, the fourth and sixth verses being supplied from other sources.)

HIGH BARBAREE

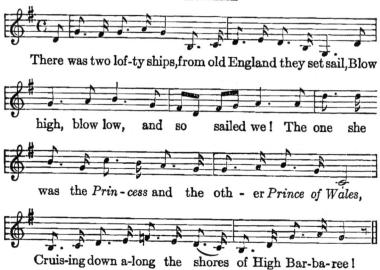

There was two lof-ty ships, from old England they set sail, Blow

high, blow low, and so sailed we! The one she

was the *Prin-cess* and the oth - er *Prince of Wales,*

Cruis-ing down a-long the shores of High Bar-ba-ree!

"Lay aloft, lay aloft," our jolly skipper cried,
"Look ahead, look astern, look a-weather and a-lee,"

"There's nothing out ahead, sir, there's nothing out astern,
There's a rock upon our quarter and a ship upon our lee,"

"Now overhaul and speak her," our jolly skipper cried;
"Are you an India merchantman or Yankee privateer?"

"I am no India merchantman or Yankee privateer,
But I am a salt-sea pirate and I'm sailing for my fee."

'Twas broadside to broadside those gallant ships did lay,
Until the *Prince of Wales* shot the pirate's masts away.

For quarter, for quarter, the pirates they did cry,
But the quarter that we gave them was to sink them in the sea.

The next was more commonly known to sailors as "Lowlands Low" than by its real title. It was originally the ballad of "Sir Walter Raleigh in the Lowlands," and will also be found in Patterson's anthology, the ship in this version being called the *Sweet Trinity*.

THE *GOLDEN VANITY*

'Twas of a lof - ty ship, boys, and she put out to sea, She goes by the name of the Gol - den Van - i - ty She's like - ly to be tak - en by a Turk - ish rov - ing ca - noe, As she sails a - long the Low - lands, Low - lands, As she sails a - long the Low-lands low!

Then up and spake our little cabin boy,
Saying "What will you give me if I will them destroy?
If I will them destroy, send them floating o'er the tide,
    And sink them in the Lowlands?"

"O the man that them destroys," the captain then replied,
"A fortune he shall have and my daughter to his bride.
A fortune he shall have and my daughter beside
    If he'll sink them in the Lowlands."

The boy bent his breast and away he jumped in,
He swam until he came to the Turkish galley-in;
He took an auger with him for to bore through her skin,
    And sink her in the Lowlands.

And some were playing cards and some were playing dice;
He bored three holes once, he bored three holes twice,
The water flow-ed in, and it dazzled their eyes,
    As they sunk in the Lowlands.

The boy swam back first upon the starboard side,
Crying "Captain, pick me up, for I'm wearied with the tide,
O Captain, pick me up, for I'm wearied with the tide,
    And I'm sinking in the Lowlands."

"I will not pick you up, you can climb up her side,
I will not pick you up," the master replied,
"I will kill you, I will shoot you, send you floating with the tide,
    And sink you in the Lowlands."

The boy swam round unto the larboard side,
Crying, "Messmates, pick me up, for I'm wearied with the tide,
O messmates, pick me up, for I'm wearied with the tide,
    And I'm sinking in the Lowlands."

His messmates picked him up, and on the deck he died.
They sewed him in his hammock which was both long and wide,
And they hove him in the sea, sent him floating with the tide,
    And sunk him in the Lowlands.

This ballad has been preserved in numberless variants both in this country and in England, and was a great favorite at sea and ashore. The Kentucky mountaineers sing a song about the *Mary Golden Tree* and the "Turkish Robbery," which contains some quaint additional verses; e.g.

    Some had hats and some had caps,
    They tried for to stop them awful water gaps.

This is the only version known to me which attempts to explain why the boy did not threaten to use his impossible weapon against his own ship.

    If it wasn't for my love for your daughter and your men,
    I would do unto you as I did unto them.

Far inland in Vermont, another version has been collected, in which the ship is the *Gold China Tree,* and her adversary a "French galilee"; which seems more likely to be encountered than a Turkish pirate on the coast of Holland. In this version the captain repents, the boy recovers, and marries the captain's daughter.

Two later ballads, also British in origin, were favorites among American crews. When a Britisher sung "Blow, Boys, Blow," in one of the versions which detailed the brutalities aboard "hard-case" Yankee ships, the Yankees would counter with the ballad of "Andrew Rose," or "Captain Rodgers' Cruelty."

ANDREW ROSE

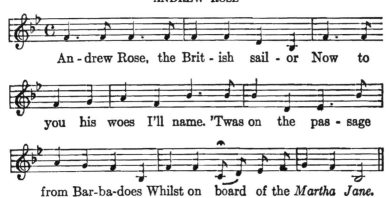

An-drew Rose, the Brit-ish sail-or Now to you his woes I'll name. 'Twas on the pas-sage from Bar-ba-does Whilst on board of the *Martha Jane.*

Chorus

Wasn't that most cruel usage,
Without a friend to interpose?
How they whipped and mangled, gagged and strangled
The British sailor, Andrew Rose.

'Twas on the quarter-deck they laid him,
Gagged him with an iron bar;
Wasn't that most cruel usage
To put upon a British tar?

'Twas up aloft the Captain sent him,
Naked beneath the burning sun,
Whilst the mate did follow after,
Lashing him till the blood did run.

The captain gave him stuff to swallow;
Stuff to you I will not name,
Whilst the crew got sick with horror,
While on board the *Martha Jane*.

'Twas in a water-cask they put him;
Seven long days they kept him there.
When loud for mercy Rose did venture,
The Captain swore no man should go there.

For twenty days they did ill-use him,
When into Liverpool they arrived.
The Judge he heard young Andrew's story;
"Captain Rodgers, you must die."

Come all ye friends and near relations,
And all ye friends to interpose;
Never treat a British sailor
Like they did young Andrew Rose.

Of the next ballad, I never heard any verses but the first, second and fourth sung on American ships. It was simply a jolly old nonsense song, to me as to those who sang it, until I chanced on the words in an old collection of broadsides. The third verse makes it perfectly plain, of course, that it was a semi-humorous ballad of transportation days; and that "Meg" had been sent to Australia as a penalty for breaking some of the laws of England. One can not but admire the true gallantry of her lover, who refrains from stating her offense!

Sing ho! for a brave and a gal - lant ship, And a

fair and fav-oring breeze, With a bul - ly crew and a

cap- tain too, To car-ry me o - ver the seas, To

car - ry me o - ver the seas, my boys, To my

true love far a - way, I'm tak - ing a trip on a

Cho.

Government ship Ten thou - sand miles a - way! Then

blow, ye winds, heigh-oh! A - rov - ing I will

go, I'll stay no more on Eng-land's shore, to

hear the mu - sic play I'm off on the morn-ing

train to cross the rag - ing main, I'm tak - ing a

trip on a Government ship, Ten thousand miles a - way!

My true love she was beautiful,
  My true love she was young;
Her eyes were like the diamonds bright,
  And silvery was her tongue,
And silvery was her tongue, my boys,
  Though now she's far away;—
She's taken a trip on a Government ship
  Ten thousand miles away.

Oh, dark and dismal was the day
  When last I seen my Meg;
She'd a Government band around each hand,
  And another one round her leg;
And another one round her leg, my boys,
  As the big ship left the bay—
"Adieu," she said, "remember me,
  Ten thousand miles away!"

I wish I were a bo'sun bold,
  Or even a bombardier,
I'd build a boat and away I'd float,
  And straight for my true love steer;
And straight for my true love steer, my boys,
  Where the dancing dolphins play,
And the whales and sharks are having their larks,
  Ten thousand miles away!

The sun may shine through a London fog,
  Or the river run quite clear;
The ocean's brine be turned to wine,
  Or I forget my beer;
Or I forget my beer, my boys,
  Or the landlord's quarter-day,
Before I forget my own sweetheart,
  Ten thousand miles away!

For the sentimental songs in the sailor's repertoire, consult any collection of "heart throbs" current ashore at the same period. One "composed" song of the last century he particularly made his own, however; and as it has more merit than most of its ilk, besides a real sea background, it will be included here.

MEDIUM CLIPPER SHIP ANDREW JACKSON

New York to San Francisco in eighty-nine days

HER BRIGHT SMILE

J. C. CARPENTER

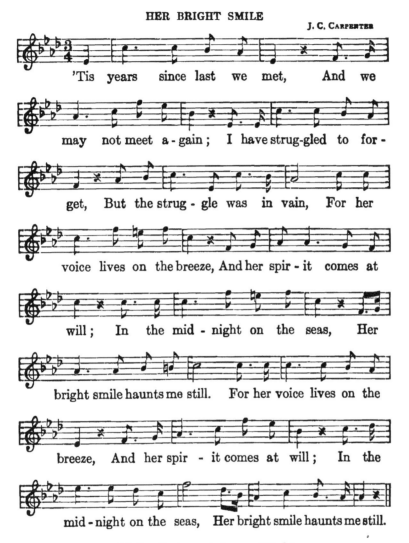

'Tis years since last we met, And we
may not meet a-gain; I have strug-gled to forget, But the strug-gle was in vain, For her
voice lives on the breeze, And her spir-it comes at
will; In the mid-night on the seas, Her
bright smile haunts me still. For her voice lives on the
breeze, And her spir-it comes at will; In the
mid-night on the seas, Her bright smile haunts me still.

At the first sweet dawn of light,
When I gaze upon the deep,
Her form still greets my sight,
While the stars their vigils keep.
When I close mine aching eyes,
Sweet dreams my senses fill,
And from sleep when I arise
Her bright smile haunts me still!

I've sailed 'neath alien skies,
I have trod the desert path,
I have seen the storm arise
Like a giant in his wrath.
Ev'ry danger I have known
That a reckless life can fill,
Yet her presence is not flown;
Her bright smile haunts me still!

Another beautiful song, but more of the "quarter-deck" than the "fore-castle" variety, was never so far as I know current ashore. The original version was a North Country ballad about the little port of Amble in Northumberland. W. E. Henley took it and rewrote it, giving it Falmouth for a home port. In the British version, the expected son "will live to serve his King, With his dirk and his hat and his little jacket blue——." That had to be changed for Yankee consumption. Whether sung by British or Americans, no song so tenderly expresses the homesick longing of the sailor in foreign parts.

HOME, DEARIE, HOME

Oh, Bos-ton's a fine town, with ships in the bay, And I

wish in my heart it was there I was to-day, I

wish in my heart I was far a-way from here, A-

sit-ting in my par-lor and talk-ing to my dear,

Then it's home, dear-ie, home, it's home I want to be,

And it's home, dear-ie, home, a-cross the roll-ing sea,

Oh, the oak and the ash and the bon-ny el-lum

tree, They're all a-grow-in' green in my

own coun-tree, Then it's home, dear-ie, home!

In Baltimore a-walking a lady I did meet,
With her baby on her arm as she walked down the street,
And I thought how I sailed, and the cradle standing ready,
And the pretty little babe that has never seen its daddy.

And if it's a girl, oh, she shall live with me,
And if it's a boy, he shall sail the rolling sea;
With his tarpaulin hat and his little jacket blue,
He shall walk the quarter-deck as his daddy used to do.

Another Boston song of quite a different caliber follows. It is copied from Capt. Whall's collection, by permission of James Brown & Sons, Glasgow.

BOSTON

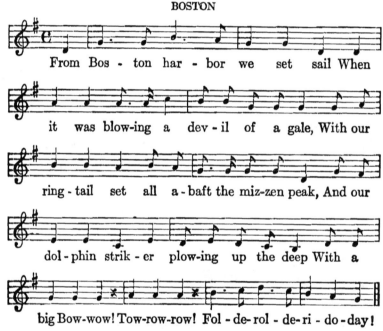

From Bos - ton har - bor we set sail When

it was blow-ing a dev - il of a gale, With our

ring - tail set all a - baft the miz-zen peak, And our

dol - phin strik - er plow-ing up the deep With a

big Bow-wow! Tow-row-row! Fol - de-rol - de-ri - do-day!

Up comes the skipper from down below,
And he looks aloft and he looks alow,
And he looks alow and he looks aloft,
And it's "Coil up your ropes there, fore and aft."

Then down to his cabin he quickly crawls,
And unto his steward he loudly bawls,
"Go mix me a glass that will make me cough,
For it's better weather here than it is up aloft."

We poor sailors standing on the deck,
With the blasted rain all a-pouring down our necks;
Not a drop of grog would he to us afford,
But he damns our eyes with every other word.

And one thing which we have to crave
Is that he may have a watery grave,
So we'll heave him down into some dark hole,
Where the sharks'll have his body and the devil have his soul.

It was singular that with all the vast pride and delight of the sailor in his ship, so few songs were sung in celebration of the qualities of individual vessels. There was one about the California clipper *Sovereign of the Seas,* which went to the same tune as the 'forty-niners' song,

Oh, Susanna, don't you cry for me,
For I'm bound to California with my washbowl on my knee.

But in spite of its being of so comparatively recent a date, I have never been able to collect more than a few tag-ends of the verses.

Oh, Susanna, darling, take your ease,
For we have beat the clipper fleet—the *Sovereign of the Seas!*

and

Holystone the cabin and get down upon your knees;
None of your lime-juice touches in the *Sovereign of the Seas!*

Only one such ballad has survived in its entirety; the grand old song of the *Dreadnaught.* The tune is a variant of an old English naval song, "The Flash Frigate," or "La Pique."

THE *DREADNAUGHT*

There is a flash pack-et, flash pack-et of fame,

She hails from New York and the *Dreadnaught's* her name,

She is bound to the west-ward, where the

storm-y winds blow, Bound a-way in the

Dread-naught to the west-ward we'll go.

Now the *Dreadnaught* is hauling out of Waterloo dock,
Where the boys and the girls to the pierhead do flock.
They give her three cheers, as the tears down do flow,
Crying "God bless the *Dreadnaught* where'er she may go!"

Now the *Dreadnaught* she lies in the river Mersey,
Awaiting the tugboat to take her to sea,
Out around the Rock Light where the salt tides do flow,
Bound away to the westward in the *Dreadnaught* we'll go.

Now the *Dreadnaught's* a-howling down the wild Irish Sea,
Her passengers merry, with hearts full of glee;
Her sailors like lions walk the deck to and fro;
She's the Liverpool packet—O Lord, let her go!

Now the *Dreadnaught* is sailing the Atlantic so wide,
Where the high roaring seas roll along her black side,
With her sails tautly set for the Red Cross to show
She's the Liverpool packet—O Lord, let her go!

Now the *Dreadnaught* is crossing the Banks of Newfoundland,
Where the water's so green and the bottom's all sand,
Where the fishes of the ocean they swim to and fro,
She's the Liverpool packet—O Lord, let her go!

And now she is sailing down the Long Island shore,
Where the pilot will board us as he's oft done before.
"Fill away your main-topsail, board your main-tack also!"
She's the Liverpool packet—O Lord, let her go!

Now the *Dreadnaught's* arriv-ed in New York once more.
Let's go ashore, shipmates, on the land we adore.
With wives and with sweethearts so happy we'll be,
And drink to the *Dreadnaught* wherever we be.

Now a health to the *Dreadnaught* and all her brave crew,
To bold Captain Samuels and his officers too;
Talk about your flash packets, Swallowtail and Black Ball,
The *Dreadnaught's* the flier that outsails them all.

Although not the fastest of the Western Ocean packets, the *Dreadnaught* was probably the best known of them all. She was built at Newburyport, Mass., in 1853, and was 1413 tons register; a very large ship for those days. During her first eight trips, her average eastern passage was 21 days 15 hours, and for the western passage, 24 days 12 hours. She once ran from Rock Light to Sandy Hook in 19 days. Captain Samuel Samuels, her commander for ten years, has published an account of his interesting career in a book entitled "From the Forecastle to the Cabin." He died in Brooklyn in 1908.

Captain Clark, in "The Clipper Ship Era," says:

"The *Dreadnaught* was strikingly handsome and well designed, though by no means a sharp ship. Her masts, yards, sails, ironwork, blocks, and standing and running rigging were of the best material, and were always carefully looked after. She was a ship that would stand almost any amount of driving in heavy weather, and her fast passages were in a measure due to this excellent quality, though mainly to the unceasing vigilance and splendid seamanship of her commander. She was wrecked in 1869, while under the command of Captain P. N. Mayhew; her crew were rescued after being adrift fourteen days in the boats, but the noble old packet ship went to pieces among the rugged cliffs and crags and roaring breakers of Cape Horn."

Another old packet-ship song tells of the hardships in winter when crossing the Western Ocean. In this and the following songs, I have made a rather unsuccessful attempt to render in the music the perverse habit of the fore-castle singer of changing the orthodox time so as to hold and accent normally unaccented syllables.

THE BANKS OF NEWFOUNDLAND

You ram-blin' boys of Liv-er-pool, I'll have ye's to be-ware, When you go in a Yan-kee pack-et ship no dun-ga-rees do wear, But have a mon-key jack-et all un-to your com-mand, For there blows some cold nor'-west-ers on the Banks of New-found-land. We'll wash her and we'll scrub her down with ho-ly-stone and sand, And we'll bid a-dieu to the Vir-gin rocks on the Banks of New-found-land.

We had one Lynch from Ballynahinch, Jimmy Murphy and Mike Moore;
It was in the winter of '72 those sea-boys suffered sore.
They pawned their clothes in Liverpool and sold them all out of hand,
Not thinking of the cold north winds on the Banks of Newfoundland.

We had one lady fair on board, Bridget Reilly was her name.
To her I promised marriage and on me she had a claim.
She tore up her flannel petticoats to make mittens for our hands,
For she could not see the sea-boys freeze on the Banks of Newfoundland.

Now, boys, we're off Sandy Hook, and the land's all covered with snow;
The tugboat will take our hawser and for New York we will tow,
And when we arrive at the Black Ball dock the boys and the girls will stand;
We'll bid adieu to packet-sailing and the Banks of Newfoundland.

(Last Chorus)

We'll wash her and we'll scrub her out with holystone and sand,
For it's whilst we're here we can't be there, on the Banks of Newfoundland!

Sung to almost the same tune was another "come-all-ye," which is of so recent date that the name of the singer survives—one Johnny Clark. The *Shenandoah,* one of the later medium clippers sailing out of New York, was under the command of Captain "Jim" Murphy, of Bath, Maine, whose name indicates his family's origin. It was his custom to hoist the Irish flag under the American ensign, as his private signal. The reference to general inebriety in the last verse must be taken with a grain of salt, as being due to poetic license on the part of Johnny Clark!

THE *SHENANDOAH*

It's of a famous American ship, for New York we are bound;
Our captain being an Irishman belonging to Dublin town,
And when he gazes on that land and that city of high renown,
It's break away that green burgee and the Harp without a Crown.

It was on the seventeenth of March we arrived in New York Bay.
Our captain being an Irishman must cele-ber-ate the day,
With the Stars and Stripes high up aloft and fluttering all around,
But underneath his monkey-gaff flew the Harp without a Crown.

Now we're bound for 'Frisco, boys, and things is runnin' wild.
The officers and the sailors all drunk, and I think they are combined.
We'll wash her and we'll scrub her down, and we'll work without a frown,
For on board of the saucy *Shenandoah* flies the Harp without a Crown.

Mention is made in the next song of the clipper *California,* though it celebrates the sailor's loves ashore rather than afloat.

THE GIRLS AROUND CAPE HORN

The famed ship *Cal - i - for - ni - a,* a
ship of high re - nown, She lay in Bos - ton
har - bor 'long-side of that pret - ty town, A -
wait - ing for our or - ders to sail far from
home, And our or - ders came for
Ri - o, boys, and then a - round Cape Horn.

When we arrived in Rio we lay there quite a while,
A-fixing up our rigging and bending our new sails.
From ship to ship they cheered us as we did sail along,
And they wished us pleasant weather while rounding of Cape Horn.

While rounding of Cape Horn, my boys, fair nights and pleasant days.
Next place we dropped our anchor was in Valparaiso Bay,
Where those Spanish girls they did roll down, I solemnly do swear
They far excel those Yankee girls with their dark and wavy hair.

They love a Yankee sailor when he goes on a spree;
He'll dance and sing and make things ring, and his money he will spend free,
And when his money it is all gone on him they won't impose;
They far excel those Liverpool girls who will pawn and steal his clothes.

Here's a health to Valparaiso along the Chile main,
Likewise to those Peruvian girls, they treated me so fine.
If ever I live to get paid off, I'll sit and drink till morn
A health to the dashing Spanish girls I met around Cape Horn.

One of the few songs arising in the China trade is the ballad of the *Dom Pedro*. This New York clipper bark, built for the coffee trade with Brazil, was later put into the China run. As is shown by the rhymes, the sailor pronunciation of the North China port was at that time "Shanghee." The crew's dissatisfaction with the food, and the captain's attempt to convince them that it is "first-class grub," is amusingly set forth in the fifth stanza.

THE *DOM PEDRO*

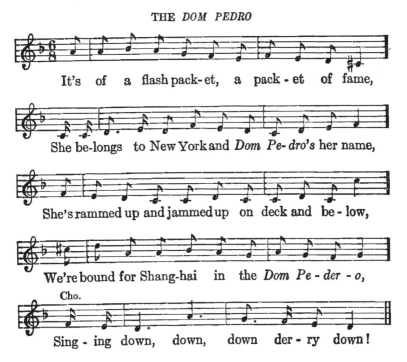

It's of a flash pack-et, a pack-et of fame,

She be-longs to New York and *Dom Pe-dro's* her name,

She's rammed up and jammed up on deck and be-low,

We're bound for Shang-hai in the *Dom Pe-der-o,*

Cho.

Sing-ing down, down, down der-ry down!

Now the pilot came down and these words he did say,
"Get ready, me boys, the ship's going away."
We braced up our yards and we gave her the slip,
And it's down Boston harbor that packet did rip.

Oh, it's now we are sailing down off of Cape Cod,
Where many a hard flashy packet has trod;
The wind it breezed up and the water did boil,
And at eight bells that night we clewed up our main royal.

And now we are sailing down on to the Line;
We catched all the rain-*water*, we had plenty of time;
We filled up our casks, as you now plainly see,
And then shaped our course for the port of Shanghai.

Now the captain is aft and he's reading a book;
He'll come for'ard bimeby and he'll growl at the cook;
He will lift up his eyes to the blessings of God
Over a plate of boiled rice and some rusty salt cod.

It's now we're arrived in the port of Shanghai;
We'll go ashore, shipmates, strange faces to see.
We'll lay up aloft and we'll furl all our sails,
Excepting the spanker that hangs in the brails.

Now our cargo's discharged and we are taking in;
We're expecting to go back to Boston ag'in;
And when we get there so jolly we'll be,
We'll be twenty merry sports all the way from Shanghai.

No collection would be complete that did not include some specimens of the negro songs which were heard whenever those accomplished singers made up part of the crew. About the negro origin of the first I am not certain; it was sung by a Frenchman; but I suspect he learned it from some one of a darker complexion. The next was sung by the crew of a coast-wise steamer; and the third "caught on" in the navy during the late war, and was sung to me by an officer on one of the destroyer squadrons.

SINDBAD

Oh, it's Sind-bad the sail-or and Rob-in-son Cru-soe, I left my na-tive coun-ter-ie a-roam-ing for to go. I went to be a sail-or, re-turned just as you see, A mix-ture of an In-di-an, a Turk, and a Jap-an-nee.

Oh, jef-fer see jee my jib-ber a-hoy, Jib-ber a ho-ry po-ry, Hi-ky-si-ky-i-ky-tike was king of the Wall-o-per Do-ry.

IN DE MORNIN'

Oh, what's de use of work-in' so hard In de morn-in'? What's de use of work-in' so hard, In de morn-in' so soon? Oh, what's de use of work-in' so hard? My gal works in a white man's yard In de morn-in', In de morn-in', so soon!

She cook dat chicken, she gimme de stuffin', (thrice)
She t'ink I'm workin', but I'm only bluffin'

She cook dat chicken, she gimme de wing, (thrice)
She t'ink I'm workin', but I ain't doin' a thing.

ROCKS IN DE MOUNTENS

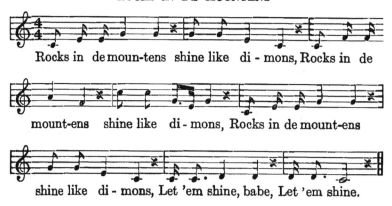

Rocks in de moun-tens shine like di-mons, Rocks in de mount-ens shine like di-mons, Rocks in de mount-ens shine like di-mons, Let 'em shine, babe, Let 'em shine.

Take dis haim-mah, gib it to de capten, (thrice)
Tell 'im I'm gone, babe, tell 'im I'm gone.

Dis same haim-mah kill Jack Johnson, (thrice)
Didn' kill me, babe, didn' kill me.

There can be little doubt that the next song, although it was sung through-out the merchant service, began life with the fishing fleet. We have the testi-mony of Kipling in "Captains Courageous" that it was a favorite within recent years of the Banks fishermen. It is known as "The Fishes" and also by its more American title of "The Boston Come-all-ye." The chorus finds its origin in a Scotch fishing song "Blaw the Wind Southerly." A curious fact is that Captain Whall, a Scotchman himself, prints this song with an entirely dif-ferent tune, and one that has no connection with the air of the Tyneside keel-men to which our own Gloucester fishermen sing it.

THE BOSTON COME-ALL-YE
(OR THE FISHES)

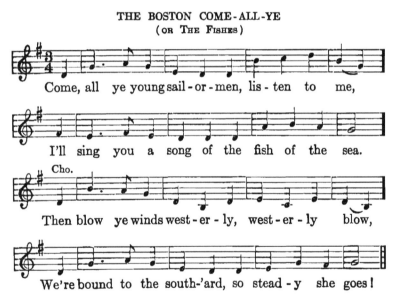

Come, all ye young sail-or-men, lis-ten to me,

I'll sing you a song of the fish of the sea.

Cho.

Then blow ye winds west-er-ly, west-er-ly blow,

We're bound to the south-'ard, so stead-y she goes!

Oh, first come the whale, the biggest of all;
He clumb up aloft and let every sail fall.

And next come the mack'rel with his strip-ed back;
He hauled aft the sheets and boarded each tack.

Then come the porpoise with his short snout;
He went to the wheel, calling "Ready! About!"

Then come the smelt, the smallest of all;
He jumped to the poop and sung out "Topsail, haul!"

The herring come saying, "I'm king of the seas,
If you want any wind, why, I'll blow you a breeze."

Next come the cod with his chuckle-head;
He went to the main-chains to heave at the lead.

Last come the flounder as flat as the ground;
Says "Damn your eyes, chuckle-head, mind how you sound!"

The whalers also celebrated their exploits in song; and although there are few left alive who can sing them, I have been able to secure some of these songs with the authentic airs to which they used to be sung. The first went to the tune of "Hail to the Chief."

THERE SHE BLOWS!

Lo, as the sun from his o-cean bed ris-ing

Wide o'er the wa-ter his glitt'-ring beam throws,

Hark! from the masthead a voice cheer'-ly cry-ing,

"Hard on our lee-beam, a whale there she blows!"

Call up your sleep-ers then, lar-board and star-board men,

Main yard a-back and your boats lower a-way,

Broad on our lee-beam, see the white wa-ter gleam,

Wreath-ing its foam in a gar-land of spray!

Lo, the leviathan in vastness is lying,
Making the ocean his voluptuous bed;
While o'er and around him the sea birds are flying,
Dark, foaming billows dash over his head.
    Now each man watch with care, there goes his flukes in air;
    Slowly but stately he sinks in the main.
    Now peak your oars a while, rest from your weary toil,
    Waiting and watching his rising again.

Now row, hearties, row as you love your salvation;
Row, hearties, row, let your reeking sweat flow.
Give to your blood a free circulation,
Bend to your oars, lads, give way all you know.
    Now see each boat advance, eager to gain first chance,
    Fleeting like shadows o'er the blue main.
    "Stand up an' give him some, send both your irons home;
    Cheerily stern all, trim the boat, give him the line."

Gallied and sore, fins and flukes in commotion,
Blackskin and boats are cleaving the spray,
While long, loud, and shrill winds his pipe o'er the ocean,
Frightened, bewildered, he brings to in dismay.
    Now haul line, every man, gather in all you can,
    As lances and spades from your thwarts clear away.
    Now take your oars again, each and every man
    As safely and surely we hold him in play.

The power of man o'er the king of the ocean
Is shown by the end when we gain our desire;
For a lance in his life creates a commotion.
Slowly he sinks with his chimney on fire.
    Hear now the glad shout, from each and every seaman out,
    Matching the billow's most turbulent roar.
    From his spouthole on high, see the red signal fly.
    Slowly he dies and the battle is o'er.

The air to the next song was taken from an old English ballad which relates the adventures of a knight and a frolicsome lady. The curious can find the original words in Percy's Reliques of Ancient Poetry under the title "The Baffl'd Knight; or, The Lady's Policy." Somewhat scandalous variants of this old ballad itself were also found in the sailor's collection of verse.

"A DEAD WHALE OR A STOVE BOAT"

Sperm whalers after their prey

The words were copied out of an old logbook in the New Bedford Public Library. No modern whaleman has been able to say what is meant by the reference to forty-four points in the whaler's compass. "Tonbas" was Tumbez, at the mouth of the Guayaquil River; the same well-known whaling rendezvous to which Admiral Porter took his fleet of captured British whalers after his South Pacific raid in 1812. "Tuckoona" was undoubtedly Talcahuano, on the Chilean coast, though the merchant sailor's pronunciation of this name was "Turkeywanna."

BLOW, YE WINDS

'Tis ad - ver -tised in Bos - ton, New York and Buf - fa - lo, Five hun - dred brave A - mer - i - cans, a - whal-ing for to go, sing-ing, Blow, ye winds in the morn - ing, And blow, ye winds, high - o! Clear a - way your run - ning gear, And blow, ye winds, high - o!

They send you to New Bedford, that famous whaling port,
And give you to some land-sharks to board and fit you out.

They send you to a boarding-house, there for a time to dwell;
The thieves they there are thicker than the other side of hell!

They tell you of the clipper-ships a-going in and out,
And say you'll take five hundred sperm before you're six months out.

It's now we're out to sea, my boys, the wind comes on to blow;
One half the watch is sick on deck, the other half below.

But as for the provisions, we don't get half enough;
A little piece of stinking beef and a blamed small bag of duff.

Now comes that damned old compass, it will grieve your heart full sore,
For theirs is two-and-thirty points and we have forty-four.

Next comes the running rigging, which you're all supposed to know;
'Tis "Lay aloft, you son-of-a-gun, or overboard you go!"

The cooper's at the vise-bench, a-making iron poles,
And the mate's upon the main hatch a-cursing all our souls.

The Skipper's on the quarter-deck a-squinting at the sails,
When up aloft the lookout sights a school of whales.

"Now clear away the boats, my boys, and after him we'll travel,
But if you get too near his fluke, he'll kick you to the devil!"

Now we have got him turned up, we tow him alongside;
We over with our blubber-hooks and rob him of his hide.

Now the boat-steerer overside the tackle overhauls,
The Skipper's in the main-chains, so loudly he does bawl!

Next comes the stowing down, my boys; 'twill take both night and day,
And you'll all have fifty cents apiece on the hundred and ninetieth lay.

Now we are bound into Tonbas, that blasted whaling port,
And if you run away, my boys, you surely will get caught.

Now we are bound into Tuckoona, full more in their power,
Where the skippers can buy the Consul up for half a barrel of flour!

But now that our old ship is full and we don't give a damn,
We'll bend on all our stu'nsails and sail for Yankee land.

When we get home, our ship made fast, and we get through our sailing,
A winding glass around we'll pass and damn this blubber whaling!

Captain Bunker, whose name occurs in the next song, was a noted sperm whaler. He died not many years ago in Sailors' Snug Harbor.

COAST OF PERU

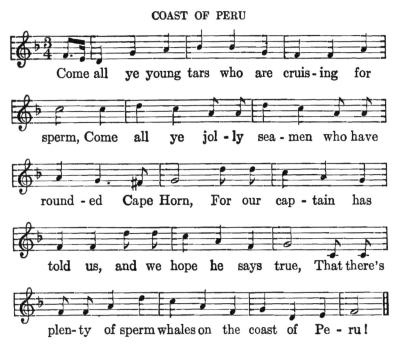

Come all ye young tars who are cruis-ing for sperm, Come all ye jol-ly sea-men who have round-ed Cape Horn, For our cap-tain has told us, and we hope he says true, That there's plen-ty of sperm whales on the coast of Pe-ru!

'Twas early one morning just as the sun rose
That a man from the mast-head sung out "There she blows!"
"Where away?" cried our captain, "and how does he lay?"
"Two points on our lee, sir; scarce three miles away."

"Then call up all hands and be of good cheer;
Get your lines in your boats and your tackle-falls clear.
Hoist and swing fore and aft; stand by, each boat's crew,
Lower away, lower away, as the main-yard swings to."

Our waist-boat got down, and of course she got the start.
"Lay me on, Captain Bunker, I'm hell for a long dart!"
Now bend to your oars and make the boat fly,
But one thing we dread of, keep clear of his eye!

Now the captain is fast and the whale has gone down,
And the first mate lies waiting his line to bend on.
Now the whale has come up, like a log he did lay;
Whatever he done, boys, he gave us fair play.

(Line missing)
But we fought him 'longside and a lance we thrust in,
Which caused the whale to vomic and the blood for to spout;
In less than ten minutes he rolled both fins out.

I have no air to the following sperm whaler's song. "Diego" was probably the island of Diego Ramirez, off Cape Horn, for which the sailor's every-day name was "The Rammerees." *

'Twas a love of adventure and a longing for gold,
    And a hardened desire to roam,
Tempted me far away o'er the watery world,
    Far away from my kindred and home.

With a storm-beaten captain, so fearless and bold,
    And a score of brave fellows or two,
Far away to the hardships, the hunger and cold,
    Sailed this fearless and jovial crew.

Have you ever cruised on Diego's bold shores,
    That are washed by the Antarctic wave,
Where the white-plumed albatross merrily soars,
    O'er many a poor whaler's grave?

Did you ever hear tell of that mighty sperm whale,
    That when boldly attacked in his lair,
With one sweep of his mighty and ponderous tail
    Sends the whaleboat so high in the air?

Did you ever join in with those heart-ringing cheers,
    With your face turned to Heaven's blue dome,
As laden with riches you purchased so dear
    You hoisted your topsails—bound home?

Also—to my deep regret—I have been unable to find any one who recalls the air to which this fine old song was sung. It was a favorite with the "bow-

* Cf. Masefield's "Song of Shipwreck."
      "It blew like the Bull of Barney, a beast of a breeze,
      'N' over the rail come the cold green lollopin' seas,
      'N' she went ashore at the dawn on the Ramirez.''

"head" whalemen, who were accustomed to put in at the Hawaiian Islands on the homeward voyage, after a season spent in hunting their prey amid the ice-floes of the Arctic.

ROLLING DOWN TO OLD MAUI *

Once more we sail with a favoring gale
   A-bounding o'er the main,
And soon the hills of the tropic clime
   Will be in view again.
Six sluggish months have passed away
   Since from your shores sailed we,
But now we're bound from the Arctic ground
   Rolling down to old Maui.

Chorus

Rolling down to old Maui, my boys,
Rolling down to old Maui,
But now we're bound from the Arctic ground,
Rolling down to old Maui.

We will heave our lead where old Diamond Head
   Looms up on old Oahu,
Our masts and rigging are covered with ice,
   Our decks are filled with snow.
The hoary head of the Sea Gull Isles
   That decks the Arctic Sea,
Are many and many leagues astern
   Since we steered for old Maui.

O welcome the seas and the fragrant breeze
   Laden with odors rare,
And the pretty maids in the sunny glades
   Who are gentle, kind and fair,
And their pretty eyes, even now look out,
   Hoping some day to see
Our snow-white sails before the gales
   Rolling down to old Maui.

* Pronounced "Mo-hee."

Once more we sail with a favoring gale
    Toward our distant home,
Our mainmast sprung, we're almost done,
    Still we ride the ocean's foam.
Our stun'sail booms are carried away,
    What care we for that sound,
A living gale is after us,
    Hurrah! We're homeward bound.

The fresh water sailormen have their own songs; and it seems fitting to include some samples here, especially as the sailing craft on which they arose have vanished as completely from the Lakes as from salt water.

THE CRUISE OF THE *BIGLER*

Now my boys if you will lis-ten, I'll sing you a
lit-tle song, So sit you down a-while here, I'll
not de-tain you long. At Mil-wau-kee in Oc-
to-ber, I chanced to get a "sit," On the tim-ber
schoon-er *Big-ler*, Be-long-ing to De-troit.

Cho.

Oh, watch her, and catch her, Jump up on her Ju-ba
Ju, Oh, give her sheet and let her rip, We're the
boys'll put her through! You ought to've seen her
howl-ing, When the wind was blow-ing free, On our
pas-sage down to Buf-fa-lo From Mil-wau-kee!

It was a Sunday morning about the hour of ten,
The *Robert Emmett* towed us into Lake Michigan.
We set sail where she left us in the middle of the fleet,
The wind was from the sou'th'ard, so we had to give her sheet.

The wind came up that night, my boys, and blew both stiff and strong,
And swiftly through Lake Michigan the *Bigler* ploughed along.
And far before her foaming bows the dashing waves she'd fling;
With every stitch of canvas set, and the courses wing and wing.

But the wind it came ahead before we reached the Manitou,
And two-and-a-half a day, sir, just suited the *Bigler's* crew,
From this into the Beavers we steered her full and by,
We kept her to the wind, my boys, as close as she could lie.

At Skillagalee* and Wabbleshanks,† the entrance to the Strait,
We might have passed the fleet ahead if they'd hove to to wait;
But we swept them all before us, the neatest ever you saw,
Clear out into Lake Huron from the Straits of Mackinaw.

At Huron Lake we passed Presqu' Isle, and then we bore away;
The wind being fair we soon flew by the Isle of Thunder Bay.
The captain ordered a sharp lookout, the night it being dark,
Our course was steering south-southwest for the light on Point aux Barques.

Now we're off of Point aux Barques, on Michigan's east shore,
A-booming for the river as we've often done before.
Abreast Port Huron light, my boys, both anchors we let go,
And the *Sweepstakes* came along and took the *Bigler* in tow.

She took the nine of us in tow, we all were fore and aft,
She towed us down to Lake St. Clair and stuck us on the flats.
The *Hunter* eased her tow-line to give us some relief,
And the *Bigler* went astern and smashed right into the *Maple Leaf.*

And then the *Sweepstakes* left us outside the river light,
Lake Erie's blustering winds and stormy waves to fight.
We laid to at the Hen and Chickens, the wind it blew a gale,
And we had to lay till morning, for we could not carry sail.

* Isle aux Galets
† Waugoshance.

We made the Eau and passed Long Point, the wind being fresh and free,
And down the Canadian shore we humped, Port Colborne on our lee.
Oh, what is that ahead of us? We knew as we drew near,
'Tis the light upon the "Dummy"; we are nigh to Buffalo pier.

Now the *Bigler* she's arriv-ed at Buffalo port at last,
And under Reed's elevator the *Bigler* she's made fast.
And in some lager-beer saloon we'll take a social glass,
We'll all be jolly shipmates, and we'll let the bottle pass.

Oh, now my song is ended, and I hope it pleases you.
Let's drink to the old *Bigler,* her officers and crew.
I hope she'll sail till kingdom come, command of Cal McKee,
Between the port of Buffalo and Mil-wau-kee.

THE *PERSIA'S* CREW

Sad and dis-mal is the tale I will re-
late to you, A-bout the schoon-er
Per-sia, her of-fi-cers and crew, Who
sank be-neath the storm-y deep, in life to
rise no more, When winds and des-o-
la-tion swept Lake Hu-ron's rock-bound shore.

They left Chicago on their lee, their songs they did resound,
And they so full of joy and glee as homeward they were bound.
They·little thought the sound of death would meet them on their way,
And they, so full of joy and glee, should in Lake Huron lay.

The sailors' names I did not know, excepting one or two.
Down in the deep they all did go; they were a luckless crew.
Not a soul escaped to land to clear the myst'ry o'er;
In watery depths they all did go, upon Lake Huron's shore.

In mystery their dooms are sealed; they did collide, some say,
But that is all to be revealed upon the judgment day.
And when the angels take their stand to wake the waters blue,
And send forth the commander of the ill-starred *Persia's* crew.

Daniel Sullivan was their mate, a man both bold and brave,
As ever was compelled by fate to fill a sailor's grave.
He will be mourned as a friend; alas! his days are o'er.
In watery depths he now doth lie, upon Lake Huron's shore.

Oh, Dan, your many friends will mourn, your fate upon them frown;
They'll wait in vain for your return back in Oswego town.
They'll miss the sly glance of your eye, your hand they'll clasp no more;
In watery depths you now do lie, upon Lake Huron's shore.

No mother's hand was there to press that brow-distracting pain;
No gentle wife was there to kiss that cold brow o'er again.
No sister or no brother nigh, no little ones to mourn;
Down in the deep they all did go, far from their friends and home.

Around Presque Isle the seagulls scream their dismal notes along,
And that is the sad requiem of the dismal funeral song.
They skim along the water blue, and then aloft they soar,
In memory of the *Persia's* crew, lost on Lake Huron's shore.

We should not close without some mention of the sailor's "rhymes for occasions." There were the "Rules of the Road at Sea," which every young sailor learned as soon as he learned to box the compass, the first for daytime, the second for night use.

RULES OF THE ROAD

I

If close hauled on the starboard tack,
No other ship can cross your track;
If on the port tack you appear,
Ships going free must all keep clear;
While you must yield, when going free,
To ships close-hauled upon your lee.
And if you have the wind right aft,
Keep clear of every sailing craft.

II

When both side lights you see ahead,
Port your helm and show your RED.
GREEN to GREEN or RED to RED,
Perfect safety—go ahead!

If to your starboard RED appear,
It is your duty to keep clear.
But when upon your port is seen
A vessel's starboard light of GREEN,
There's nothing much for you to do,
For GREEN to port keeps clear of you!

There were his weather rhymes in great store:

Winds that change against the sun
Are always sure to backward run.

And of the barometer,

First rise after a low,
Squalls expect and more blow.

Of sunset and sunrise,

Red at night,
Sailor's delight.
Red in the morning,
Sailor's warning.

Of winds and clouds,

> First the rain and then the wind,
> Topsail sheets and halliards mind;
> First the wind and then the rain,
> Hoist your topsails up again.

and

> Mackerel skies and mares' tails
> Make tall ships carry low sails.

There was his grace before meat, when the beef-kids came in from the galley:

> Old horse! old horse! how came you here?
> —From Sacarap' to Portland Pier.
> I carted stone this many a year,
> Until, worn out by sore abuse,
> They salted me down for sailors' use.
> The sailors they do me despise;
> They turn me over and damn my eyes,
> Cut off my meat and pick my bones,
> And heave the rest to Davy Jones.

And these were the rhymes for turning out the watch, which were sometimes chanted at the forecastle door:

> Awake, awake, you weary sleepers,
> Know you not 'tis almost day?
> Here while thus you're sleeping,
> God's best hours will pass away.

> Show a leg! Show a leg!

In the second rhyme, the terms "larbowlin" and "starbowlin" are old names for the port and starboard watches respectively.

> Larbowlins stout, you must turn out
>   And sleep no more within;
> For if you do we'll cut your clew,
>   And let starbowlins in.

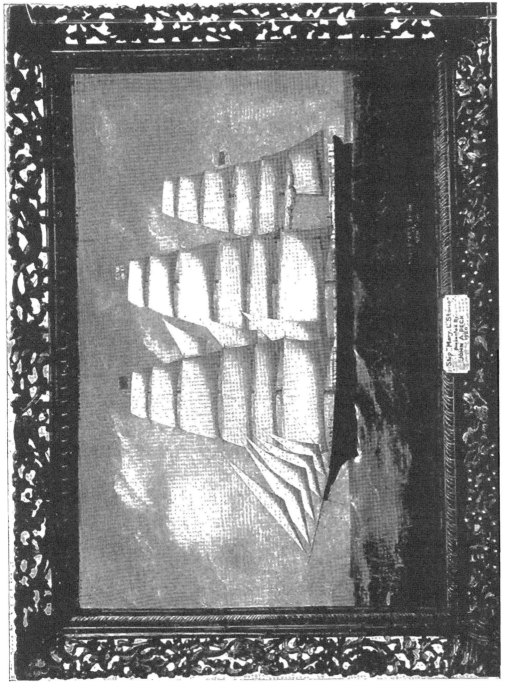

SHIP MARY L STONE

A late type of American merchantman, built for cargo-carrying as well as speed

And with this we bid farewell to the Singing Sailor. He went his way with the ships he loved and served. No roadstead resounds any more with Santy Anna or Rio Grande, while the men tramp round the capstan and the cable clanks into the lockers under their feet. No yards rise swaying to the tune of Whiskey Johnny; nor does the invocation to Paddy Doyle aid bleeding fingers to furl the steel-hard canvas as the ship goes plunging through a Cape Horn night. *Autre temps, autre mœurs;* and steam asks no help from song. "The ships have gone, and the men left the employ," but a nation which has come to value its maritime history and traditions should not forget these songs, rude and artless though they may be, for they were a living part of the glory of the days of sail.

CHANTEYS

These are the songs that we sing with crowding feet,
    Heaving up the anchor chain,
Or walking down the deck in the wind and sleet
    And in the drizzle and rain.

These are the songs that we sing beneath the sun,
    Or under the stars of night,
And they help us through with the work to be done
    When the moon climbs into sight.

These are the songs that tell our inmost hopes
    While we pull and haul amain,
The bo'sun booming as we lean with the ropes,
    And we, bringing in the refrain.

                        —*Harry Kemp.*

LIST OF SONGS

I. SHORT-DRAG SHANTIES

PAGE

Boney (John Franswor)............ 2

Haul Away Joe.................... 3

Haul on the Bowline.............. 4

PAGE

Paddy Doyle 4

Johnny Boker 5

II. HALYARD SHANTIES

Whiskey Johnny 6

Blow, Boys, Blow................. 7

Black Ball Line, The............. 9

Blow the Man Down (1)........... 10

Blow the Man Down (2)........... 11

Blow the Man Down (3, with music). 14

Juley 15

Sing Sally O.................... 16

Liza Lee 16

Shallo Brown 17

Goodbye, My Love, Goodbye........ 17

Roll the Cotton Down............. 18

Lower the Boat Down............. 18

Poor Old Man (The Old Horse; The

Dead Horse Shanty)............ 19

Run With the Bullgine........... 19

Alabama 20

Long Time Ago, A................ 20

Hundred Years on the Eastern Shore,

A 22

Huckleberry Hunting 23

Reuben Ranzo 24

Tom's Gone to Hilo.............. 25

Hanging Johnny 27

So Handy 28

Cheer'ly Man 29

Drunken Sailor, The (Early in the

Morning) 30

III. WINDLASS OR CAPSTAN SHANTIES

Sally Brown 32

Shenandoah (The Wide Missouri)... 33

Santy Anna (Plains of Mexico).... 34

Rio Grande 35

A-Roving (Maid of Amsterdam).... 37

Stormalong (Old Stormy)......... 38

Rolling King (South Australia).... 39

Heave Away (We're All Bound to Go) 40

Slav Ho! 42

Clear the Track................. 43

Lowlands (1) 44

Lowlands (2) 45

Johnny Come Down to Hilo........ 46

John Cherokee 47

Hog Eye Man..................... 48

Sacramento (Banks of Sacramento;

Doo-da-day) 49

Paddy Works on the Railway....... 51

Can't You Dance the Polka? 52

O You Santy..................... 53

Goodbye, Fare You Well (Homeward

Bound) 54

One More Day.................... 55

Fire Down Below................. 56

Mobile Bay 57

Across the Western Ocean......... 57

Leave Her, Johnny (Time for Us to

Leave Her) 58

117

IV. FORECASTLE SONGS

PAGE

Stately Southerner, The (The Yankee
    Man-of-War; The Ranger)........ 61
Ye Parliament of England.......... 63
Constitution and Guerrière, The..... 65
Jamestown Homeward Bound, The... 67
Derby Ram (The Ram of Derby; The
    Old Tup) 68
Captain Kidd 69
.Flying Cloud, The................. 73
Greenland Fishery (The Whale)..... 76
High Barbaree 78
Golden Vanity, The (Lowlands Low) 79
Andrew Rose (Captain Rodgers'
    Cruelty) 81
Ten Thousand Miles Away.......... 83
Her Bright Smile................. 85
Home, Dearie, Home............... 87

PAGE

Boston 88
Dreadnaught, The 90
Banks of Newfoundland, The........ 92
Shenandoah, The 93
Girls Around Cape Horn, The....... 94
Dom Pedro, The 95
Sindbad 97
In de Mornin' 98
Rocks in de Mountens............. 98
Boston Come-All-Ye, The (The Fishes) 99
There She Blows! 101
Blow, Ye Winds 103
Coast of Peru 105
'Twas a Love of Adventure........ 106
Rolling Down to Old Maui.......... 107
Cruise of the Bigler, The........... 109
Persia's Crew, The 111

CPSIA information can be obtained
at www.ICGtesting.com
Printed in the USA
BVHW010724141119
563722BV00004B/60/P